POINTS *for a* COMPASS ROSE

POINTS *for a* COMPASS ROSE

Evan S. Connell

COUNTERPOINT
BERKELEY

Copyright © 2012 Evan S. Connell. All rights reserved under
International and Pan-American Copyright Conventions.

First published in Great Britain by Vintage, 1992.

Library of Congress cataloging-in-Publication Data is available.

ISBN: 978-1-61902-022-1

Interior design by David Bullen
Cover design by Ann Weinstock

COUNTERPOINT
1919 Fifth Street
Berkeley, CA 94710
www.counterpointpress.com

Distributed by Publishers Group West

Printed in the United States of America

10   9   8   7   6   5   4   3   2   1

to Gale Garnett

POINTS *for a* COMPASS ROSE

*L*ET ME BEGIN my story like all true myths
with the statement that I never knew my parents.
Next, permit me to describe myself. My features,
unless I feel animated, express indolence and sloth.
My mouth with its moist sensual lips usually hangs open
because I have trouble breathing through my nose.
My small brown eyes gaze inward. As you can guess,
I spend my days alone—to say nothing of the nights.
Do you know who I am?

A teacher of classical drama might criticize me
for addressing you intimately, and point out that
the poet should pretend to be talking to himself
or to somebody else. But I'm sick of old devices.

Listen. I've decided to take a trip. I'm going to Padua
like Mikolaj Kopernik to study Achellini's cosmography;
like Andreas Vesalius to visit the master anatomists;
like Albrecht Dürer to Firenze. I don't plan to return
altogether ignorant, and you're welcome to join me.
So what do you say? Come along. Let's travel together.
God our suzerain has a duty to protect His vassals;
but with Him or without we'll go back and forth
along the dusty ways choosing all knowledge
as our provenance. Interspersing fact with lore,
interpreting experience in terms of moral purpose,
we can adopt the method of our medieval predecessors.

Only don't forget: those who go on pilgrimages
seldom become saints. Do you understand?

Look. My uncle is designing a cathedral
although he's not been sponsored by any church.
When people ask who's to pay for the material
he dismisses the question, because in his view
the visible world is nothing but a reflection
of some incomprehensible spiritual order.
Is that clear?

Let me put it this way. I quote the Governor of Bithynia,
Pliny the Younger, as he writes uneasily to Trajan
for advice on how to negotiate with Christians.
I have never participated in interrogations . . .
Thus he begins, the rest of the letter testifying
to his distress and bewilderment. Trajan responds
majestically that Christians ought to be punished
although he does not think they need be hunted,
which means that he doesn't consider them a threat.
How little Emperors perceive.

Clement Attlee was the Prime Minister of England
who concurred with President Truman's decision
to annihilate Hiroshima. However, 16 years later
Attlee wrote: *We knew nothing whatever at the time*
about the genetic effects of an atomic explosion.
I knew nothing about fall-out and all the rest . . .
Yet H. J. Muller had won the Nobel Prize in 1927
for investigating the genetic effects of radiation.
Are we not ruled by cliques of men as uninformed
as Palestinian shepherds?

Biologists who discovered radiostrontium in burns
suffered by animals exposed to atomic tests in Nevada
understood quite well the sinister quest of strontium
for bone; but their investigations were restricted,
classified under the code name "Operation Sunshine"
and units of strontium labeled "Sunshine Units."
Now do you see what I mean?

Look. High-level radioactive wastes may persist
for thousands of years. Much of this garbage
—nobody knows how much—is buried in areas
called "Farms." Maybe you don't mind being deceived,
but I bitterly resent it. Hatred nourishes me.

Gentlemen, we have been adv . . .

Toads hop out of their mouths;
snakes dangle from their nostrils.

Frost must be correct: doomed to broken careers
we should abide our incompleteness. Still
disobedience offers some choice. Take your pick.

This legend in gilded letters on the tower
of Königsberg's green gate might guide you:
Vultus fortunae variatur imagine lunae:
Crescit, decrescit, constans persistere nescit.
It means that the face of fortune varies
and knows not how to remain steadfast.

Fine dust settles on fragments of the past, my friend;
not one of us can guess what happens next.

My mother used to say I had about me an uncommon
dreaminess, which made me indifferent to the future.
She was right, of course. But as Vergil wrote:
each is attracted by his own special pleasure.

My brother, with the natural affability of genius,
graciously permits children to climb on his back
and fools to pick his brains. As for myself,
less gifted, I can abide neither. Like Socrates
my brother can follow arguments where they lead.
Beautiful, alight with wisdom and goodness
he reminds me of Odin's son Balder—reputedly
the one perfect being—because of his reluctance
to conclude anything. Or of the musician Ives
spending years on some intricate symphony
he never meant to finish. *Trahit sua quemque . . .*

You probably realize that ideas interpenetrate
just as galaxies are able to pass through each other,
while bold analogies occur to percipient men
like a celestial tide. I'll give you an example.
Listen. Nobody denies that the spider spins a web
out of its venomous self, or that good wine sours
in an ugly glass.

Here's another. Ethiopians are black Saracens;
Chingis Cham was slain by a thunderclap.

The Danube is guarded by a swarm of bees; in Damascus
Christians' bloody heads lie about the marketplace
more numerous than watermelons.

This reminds me of Richard Coeur de Lion
demonstrating the edge of his sword to Saladin
by savagely hacking a bar of iron in half.
Then the Moslem displayed his scimitar
by tossing a cushion in the air and quartering it
without a sound. This was to be expected, of course,
because Arab astronomers had been calculating
equinoctial precession and the angle of the ecliptic
while Europeans were interpreting a fanciful sky
decorated with goats, bulls, crabs and fishes.

My son thinks I'm obsessed by forgotten affairs.
I've tried to explain that love of the antique
for its own sake isn't the reason, nor conceit
nor a feeling of condescension, but some urge
to know how Man conducts himself—how he became
what he is—to trace his arduous descent
through innumerable thickets to the present.
I'd like to rediscover us in our first pleasure
and pain, in our bewilderment and creative effort,
success, wretched failure and all the rest.
I doubt if he understood. So much the worse;
maybe he'll catch up with me, maybe he won't.
I'll wait for nobody.

Take humanity's ubiquitous interest in business:
Saracens, observing how the Crusaders coveted plumes
for their helmets, opened ostrich farms in Egypt.

Glass was manufactured by Egyptians and Phoenicians
long before Christ, yet this lucrative art was neglected
by the Greeks. Why? Various answers have been suggested
but perhaps the most obvious explanation is overlooked
because we have trouble imagining patterns of thought
which exclude profit. Put it like this: the Greeks,
sensuous as they were, might have considered glass
rather unpleasant—brittle, monotonous, odorless,
devoid of texture—an odd substance admittedly useful
but disagreeable.

A single pound of Phoenician purple silk, by the way,
which once cost the equivalent of $30,000
can now be quickly and inexpensively reproduced
with a few aniline derivatives. So much for commerce.

Carved on a rock not far from Rio de Janeiro
is this message: *We are of the land of Canaan*
in Syria. We are pursued by misfortune.
It is terrible to be cast up. We have not long
to live. Despair has seized us. What despair.
Soon we shall see the ninth year of our sojourn.
Unbearable heat reigns. The water we find
is bad to drink. How accursed is the land.
Fever consumes us. It is a glowing oven.
We have no consolation other than Baal.
A forgery, according to the Brazilian Ministry
of Education. But opinions differ. It's possible
that these castaways were Carthaginian merchants
blown off course by strong winds, or perhaps
citizens who fled the Roman invaders in 146 B.C.
Whether or not the inscription is legitimate
I'll let you decide; all I know is that Africans
did land among the Azores at a very early date
and the current of human exploration runs west.

The Hindus never established colonies or sent out fleets
yet Sanscrit maps and books written centuries ago
describe in elaborate detail the coast of England.
How can this be explained? We know quite a lot,
but many things steadily elude us.

Coins minted during the reign of Diocletian
have been found in Iceland.

The ordinary pineapple, *Bromelia ananassa*,
is reputed to be of American origin.
Why is it represented with singular exactitude
on Assyrian monuments?

Olmecs at the dawn of Mesoamerican civilization
modeled ceramic figurines of dogs running on wheels
attached to their feet by wooden axles, remarkably
similar to those discovered in Mesopotamian tombs.

The word *maize* for Indian corn is derived from *mahiz*
which is the plant's name in the Haitian language.
Yet, strange to tell, the word *mayse* signifies bread
in the Lettish and Livonian tongues of northern Europe;
furthermore, the word *maise* means food in Irish,
and in old High German we find that *maz* is meat.
So the Spanish *maíz* probably antedates Colombus,
testifying to some much earlier communication.

What's the use of such useless knowledge? Listen.
You might as well ask the purpose of crystals,
maíz-pinto and feathers. We have many senses.

Some say the preeminent cause of all that we perceive
is nothing that can be perceived by human intelligence.
For example, together with perfectly comprehensible
Rhodesian cliff paintings we occasionally encounter
an abstract pattern—a double cross inside a circle.
This design also has been found in Tibetan monasteries
and early Christian churches. Called the sunwheel,
it actually predates the wheel; thus its origin

could not have been the external world. It represents
a psychic experience, and suggests men's struggles
to give their intimations abiding form. *Videmus
nunc per speculum in aenigmate.*

Where we encounter obscurity too deep for reason
it's good to sit down with description, periphrasis
or adumbration. So we are advised in wonderful prose
by Sir Thomas Browne. I'd remind you, however,
that our faculties transmit intelligible information
only so long as our reasoning strictly limits itself
to the limited conditions of our birth.

I would also remind you that intuitive thought
is not merely satisfying but necessary. If you doubt this
be good enough to account for the sudden deviations
of shoals of minnows, or a wheeling flock of birds.

How would you explain the talent of a water diviner?
The phenomenon depends on an area of small dimension
in the elbow, some say, which seems to be founded
on resonance or paranormal sensibility.

How can you explain the fact of Bonaparte's portrait
at Arcola resembling a bourgeois Etruscan head
on a late sarcophagus? Because ethnic types persist
century after century? Do you think that's sufficient?

Why do pearls lose luster when their owner dies?
Moisture of the living skin prevents them drying out,
of course. But is there another reason?

Why does the earth rotate more slowly in March
than in September?

Why was a dove seen flying from Jeanne d'Arc's mouth
at the instant of death?

What about the optic lens found in the rubble of Babylon?

Can you explain why the fatal influences of master planets
were altered by Jesus?

If it's true that balsa rafts sailed across the Pacific
many generations ago, why is there such a conspicuous
lexical poverty in the ancient Quechua language of Peru
on the subject of seamanship?

Well, it would be easy to continue
but if we've traveled this far together
I assume you understand. What I suggest,
my friend, is that we may be no wiser
than some household cat aimlessly wandering
through its master's library, which pauses
to observe his books yet has no idea what they mean.

Raymond Lully tried to define the inexplicable
by the use of a frame with unequal revolving
concentric disks subdivided into sectors
with Latin words. Such is the progress of vanity.
But what a man loves, that he clings to
and everything obstructing his way he despises,
lest he be deprived of what he loves.
I learned this from St. Maximus the Confessor.

None of us, I think, can suitably express what occurs;
it defies comprehension. Murshid ibn Munquidh,
Emir of Shaizar, for example, copied the Koran
43 times, always adding his meditations
which were different each time. *Allahu akbar.*

Incidentally, when Arab chroniclers praise someone
they praise first, as a rule, the man's piety
and next the elegance of his style—his grace
in prose, the art by which he reveals himself.

Now, here's something that can be interpreted
at least two ways, according to the context
or to the listener's predilection: Sennacherib
was beaten to death with statuettes of the gods.

Mani, the liberal Persian reformer
who accepted each of the great religions
with its various gods, including Satan,
was crucified because of his tolerance.
Doesn't that sound familiar?

Origen was tortured in Caesarea
so carefully that he was unable to die;
but according to Eusebius
he appeared strangely joyful,
as though he had experienced it once before!

I believe the influence of Plotinian doctrine
on our thought is manifest: since all things
have their origin in God, they'll be brought back
after their dispersion to live again in Him.

Now the boy approaches, swinging the censer
as it swung in adoration of Bacchus.
I reflect that the cassock of the priest
comes from Persia, his veil and tonsure
from Egypt. Alb and chasuble are prescribed
by Numa Pompilius, the stole borrowed
from a sacrificial victim, the white surplice
described by Ovid. Formulae for the exorcism
of spirits derive from Chaldean magicians.

Hilka! Hilka! Besha! Besh . . .

Lat. 22.05 N.; Long. 51.10 W.
Time moves indolently for travelers.
Seabirds accompany us.

Three days out of Bristol and few clouds.
Our course is set for an island called Brazylle
which we hear lies somewhere west of Ireland.
God protect us henceforth. July 15th, 1480.

Pots of blackamoor coins have been dug up
in the Azores, this much we accept;

about other matters we have doubts.
They say men live in far-off regions
past Gibraltar. It sounds wild and implausible.
We have doubts, too, about our Captain's purpose.

We suspect giantesses live beneath the sea,
just as we know dragons wait in grave mounds
and Valkyries eat corpses on battlefields.

We know Ran traps seafarers in her net
as inexorably as the jaws of the god Aegir
close across the prows of venturesome ships;
but if sailors have gold enough in their pockets
Ran bids them welcome to her underwater hall.

Gold, we believe, clusters at the center of the earth
like colonies of lobster. It's true our thoughts rise
and swoop on tales of gold as passionately as seagulls
which espy morsels of bread; but poor men are too poor
to afford embarrassment.

August 5th. Much apprehension. The sky overcast.
Not long since a fiery spider passed just above,
and by now the terrible thing has got to Blackpool.
Thus we lie awake, wondering and discussing our wives.

Friday. Last night sighted the North Star
but unable to fix its altitude with quadrant
or astrolabe. West by southwest we hold course
and have sailed already a thousand leagues
meeting nothing but monstrosities. One after another
we fall sick. With failing convictions we wait.
The vessel wallows and lunges.

More than any other death we fear drowning.
What could rest or sleep in these voracious wells?

What false ideals betray and humiliate
and suck at us?
Pater noster, qui es in coel . . .

Midnight. Unable to sleep.
I'll play a little on my flute.

Rain stopped. Breeze from the west,
it blows colder. Sick, alone,
an invalid propped up in bed dreaming,
I pretend and pretend and pretend.

Say I'd lived centuries ago
secluded in a cloister
enjoying beatific visions,
communing with saints,
working a miracle or two
in my spare time. What a thought!
Faber quisque fortunae suae.
I might have imagined a new Order,
after death found myself canonized
by a Church of whose faith
I had been the greatest champion
and of whose tenderness the exemplar.
Oh, it's bitter to be born late.

2:45 A.M. Why set myself against things that are?
In an age when other artists required adventure
Botticelli contrived to live without excitement.
I'll ignore the urgency of this lunatic period,
indulge my wishes, startle unsuspecting strangers
with verses of fabulous elegance, re-create daydreams,
clap at fanciful objects. Oh! By the way, my friend,
have I told you my name? I'm the Turk, Roses Bey,
who never looked at a woman but passed his life
traveling in search of fabulous flowers.

It's natural, I maintain, for an artist such as myself
to be concerned with flowers. As I pick flowers
I take them from the pattern promised by Nature;
and after I have arranged them they reveal a dignity
corresponding to that within the arranger.

The truth of Ikebana, as you may know,
is the truth of every art;
and vital creations
are understood by exceptional people.

Listen. They'll tell you in Japan
that the taste of a fruit means less
than the beauty of its blossom.

In Germany you'll be taught that 4,000 autumnal crocuses
are necessary to concoct a single ounce of saffron,
much esteemed as medicine. Nuremberg pharmacists
are buried alive if convicted of adulterating it.
Well! All we can say is that appearance passes,
truth abides. *Schein vergeht, Wahrheit besteht.*

Imperceptibly I familiarize myself with the process
of my thought, which demonstrates its own logic.
Deviations grow apparent. The tusk of the elephant
exhibits past stages, the nautilus adds chambers
to its shell, the turtle adds laminae to its plates.

I'm aware of whispering; I follow your movements.
Without knowledge the mystic sees, and you and I
are less unlike than you suspect.
Remember. Nothing that concerns us
ever wholly loses its relevance
—no language we've spoken, no oracle
or dream. Nothing. Does this make sense?

Look. High in the Andes are two piles of stone
between which somebody centuries ago strung a cord
to catch and hold the sun in its path. Do you understand?

Let me put it this way. As the parallels of geometry
intersect at infinity, so our two parallels cross
in the immutability of Man—to whom the gods granted
that he should be the measure of all things,
their beginning and their end.

Has not the rain a rhythm of its own?
Hasn't the wind some harmony?

Listen. From astrologers, magicians and alchemists
we learn a universal language and the royal art
of symbols, enabling us to sublimate reality
in favor of our true commencement. Is that clear?
No? I'll try just once more.

Symbols outlive eras and the close of civilizations.
Fresh generations become fascinated by them
and cause them to migrate—from Mesopotamia
to Cambodia, for example. Oblivious to time
they live from the 3rd millennium before Christ
to the 2nd millennium after His death. Changeless
in form, they are receptacles willing to receive
and contain the essence of new meaning. Multitudes
pour into symbols the substance of their hearts
and imaginations; invariably they lend themselves
without comment to the service of diverse functions.
In other words, they recapitulate by reiteration
our glorious adventure.

Look. The colors of a chessboard represent
our two conditions, which are Life and Death,
while the various pieces symbolize men of this world
who share a common birth, occupy different stations,
hold diverse titles, contend together and finally
experience a mutual fate leveling all ranks.
Specifically, the Queen moves aslant because
Woman is greedy and not to be trusted. The Rook
represents itinerant justices who travel across the realm;
his move is direct because a judge must deal fairly.
When we come to the Knight we find his move compounded
of the file and of the rank; the former
betokening his legal power to collect rent,
the latter his numerous extortions. Now the King,
as you may know, moves in all directions
because he is law. As to the Aufins, they are prelates
wearing horns, who move in an oblique manner;

the explanation for this is that through cupidity
almost every bishop misuses his office. Lastly
the pawns, who are poor men. Their move is short
but straight, except when they seize something,
just as a poor man moves unless stung by ambition.

Play warily, my friend, your opponent is subtle.
Take abundant thought of your moves, because the stake
is your immortal soul.

P-K4.
P-K3.

The fate of the New World was influenced by chess. Listen.
Columbus, whose petition had been consistently rejected
by the Spanish monarchs, decided to make one last attempt;
but it so happened that he arrived while King Ferdinand
was preoccupied with a game and in danger of losing.
Exasperated by the interruption, Ferdinand dismissed him.
Columbus left at once and started toward Palos de Moguer,
convinced that he would not be granted Spanish patronage.
But a certain royal attendant—Hernando del Pulgar,
who was deft at the game and sympathetic to the explorer,
murmured to Queen Isabella how the king could save his rook;
and she, leaning aside, whispered this move to the sovereign.
As a result, Ferdinand salvaged the game. Then, flattered
by his court's compliments, he sent word that a horseman
should overtake Columbus and bring him back. So you see
we ought never to despise fortuitous circumstances;
trifling in aspect, sometimes they prove momentous.

Galen and Hippocrates, incidentally, prescribe chess
for patients suffering from erysipelas.

Although early manuscripts attribute the origin
of this baffling game to Aristotle, no one knows
absolutely. It may have been devised by Sissa,
a Brahman at the palace of the Rajah Balhait
who had been requested to contrive something
which might demonstrate the values of prudence,

diligence, foresight and knowledge, thus
opposing the fatalistic implication of *nard*.
According to the legend, Balhait so enjoyed it
that he invited Sissa to select his own reward;
and the wise man said he wanted very little,
only some grains of corn on a chessboard,
to be distributed by mathematical progression.
On the first square, he said, a single grain.
On the second square, two grains. On the third,
four. On the fourth, twice that many. And so on
to the sixty-fourth and final square. Nothing else.
Balhait then ordered grain brought and measured
according to this innocent Brahman's wishes,
but before they reached the thirtieth square
all the grain of India would have been exhausted.
Sissa explained to Balhait that the required amount
would cover the earth to a depth of nine inches.
In other words: 18,446,744,073,709,551,615 grains.
You may not care about such stories, but I do;
I'm always on the lookout for instruction.

Some people disregard legends, myths, abstractions,
symbols and nightmares, but I'll tell you something.
Listen. Whoever speaks in primordial languages
speaks with a thousand tongues. He elevates
and lifts that which he treats from the individual
and transitory toward the eternal; he exalts
our personal lot to the lot of Man, releasing
in us those ineffable forces that enable humanity
to rescue itself from the grip of unspeakable events.

Here's a parable. The god of gardens and vineyards
whom the Thracians call Hero is depicted as a knight.
Iris flowers beneath the hooves of his horse
and wherever he glances the air brightens with birds.
His clothing smells of honey, early spring bees
hover around him. His sheathed sword has rusted,
wild creatures obey his command. Brambles part,
blossoms bend toward him and the desert blooms
at his approach. Can you interpret it? No? Patience.
Patience. Whatever puzzles you will be resolved.

Treblinka: 731,800. Can you guess what this means?
The forces of destruction are superbly organized.

It's been a long time, of course,
and you might prefer to forget.
Suit yourself. I don't forget anything.
Chacun à son goût, say the French.

I've watched middle-aged German tourists
pause beside those bronze plaques on the quai
just long enough to translate the inscription
before wandering along, comfortable faces
assiduously vacant. It's a weakness I have,
making notes.

I've jotted down a trifle
scratched on the wall of a dungeon
at the tip of Isle St.-Louis:
J'ai reve tellement fort de toi.
J'ai tellem...

I also note that when the Commandant of West Point,
Major General Samuel Koster, was court-martialed
for complicity in the murder of Vietnamese civilians
he was enthusiastically applauded by his cadets.

Now, suppose we take a quick look at the Aztecs.
This astonishing civilization may be understood
only if we recall that they considered themselves
children of the sun who were obligated to maintain
the life of the sun in its perpetual struggle
against the forces of Night. That is to say, Evil.
Naturally, to meet such a profound obligation
prisoners were in constant demand as sacrifices,
which called for a practiced and powerful army.

Next, the Great Wall. This interminable structure,
the most stupefying demon screen ever conceived,
was meant to shield the kingdom against low-flying devils
from the north—malignant creatures at times visible

but frequently invisible. More recently it functioned
as the model for that electronic barrier across Vietnam
proposed by our Secretary of Defense, Robert McNamara.

Not much is new. Diverse men enjoy diverse recreations.
Domitian, we are told, would waste hours catching flies;
Augustus liked to play with nuts.

Delirious emirs and sheikhs, having captured the Mongol
General Kitbuga at Ain Julud, enjoyed a round of polo
with his head.

Is violence Man's natural penumbra?

Listen. I heard on the radio this afternoon
that 20 waves of fighter bombers had attacked
the Hai Ba Trung area southeast of Hanoi,
damaging a biscuit factory.

In Hanoi's Vandien suburb two days ago
rockets struck the waterworks;
last week it was the leper hospital.

So far the United States has expended 27 billion pounds
of explosives in North and South Vietnam, Cambodia, and
Laos. Let me put it another way: 97,000 pounds per square mile.

Listen. On the 27th of July, 1656
Baruch Spinoza was excommunicated
with these words: *Let him be accursed*
by day, and accursed by night;
let him be accursed in his lying down,
and accursed in his rising up;
accursed in going out and accursed
in coming in. May the Lord
never more pardon or acknowledge him;
may the wrath and displeasure of the Lord
burn henceforth against this man,
load him with all the curses written
in the Book of the Law, and blot out

his name from under the sky.
Do you follow me?

Questions are necessarily easier than answers
but some things we can establish. For instance,
the desire for happiness is less imperative
than a lust for others' misery.

The Athenian painter Parrhasius,
having decided to represent Prometheus,
bought an old man and tortured him
to study agony's changing features.

Holy familiars at the time of the Spanish Inquisition
learned that a noose could be tightened to any degree
by means of a stick, and the stick secured with a hook.
Usually a prisoner was allowed just enough air to stay alive,
in which condition his shuddering struggles for breath
excited the excretory and sexual organs. Solicitous priests
then came to examine or console the victim, one after another,
each priest according to his interest. *Mirabile dictu!*

Portuguese missionaries to Africa in the 15th century,
horrified at the Benin human sacrifices, attempted
to introduce Christianity, but without much success.
The Benin, however, were fascinated by the missionaries'
crucifixes and added the idea to their repertoire.

De Soto, anxious to impose Christian theology on America,
introduced burning at the stake.

Historians disagree as to whether scalping
was imported from Europe or evolved independently.
The custom can be traced as far back as Herodotus
who speaks of Scythians scalping their enemies,
and Saxons and Franks busily collected scalps
during the 9th century. The Germans, of course,
practiced it. But that's irrelevant. All we know
for certain is that the New World's indigenous
citizens, with or without European advisers,

seem to have grown quite proficient
at abusing and tormenting their neighbors.

Why members of the Iroquois Confederacy,
engaged in a deadly struggle with the English,
should have voted to make war on the Algonquins
who were their only possible allies, nobody can guess.
Perhaps, like other nations before and after them,
the Iroquois were so excited by dreams of conquest
that they failed to recognize their true enemy.

The genesis of a war between technological nations
very seldom can be traced to popular folly. As a rule
its cause is some deep perversion of administrative
process. In the sordid case of Nazi Germany
the psychopathology of personnel was manifest;
in the United States it appears that responsible
administrators were misinformed, quite consciously
and with malice.

Seldom do the guilty fail to find their rhetoric.
I remember a Spokesman who, after clearing his throat,
acknowledged our presence and began: *Gentlem* . . .
Do you think it was rude of me to walk out?
Are you aware that 1 public relations expert
is employed by the Pentagon for every 2 senators?

Well, mixed diseases have mixed remedies. Time
nourishes knowledge, and daily experience teaches
facts of which our predecessors lay ignorant.
Hippocrates, for example, coming to visit Democritus
at Abdera, found him with a book open on his knee
and all around him the dead carcasses of animals
he'd dissected to locate the source of an illness
—in this case Melancholy. The surgery didn't work
but how many of our physicians have shown more insight?
Stupefying problems beset us, and solutions look
more plentiful than satisfactory. Spiders go skating
across the surface of a pond with greater engagement
than men probe the origin of their troubles.

It's hard to describe what puzzles us, true;
yet we have on record a list of accomplishments
which would encourage us. Crolius, as you may know,
devised volatile gold—a fulminate imitating thunder
and lightning that explodes louder than gunpowder.
Cornelius has given form to inextinguishable light,
perpetual motion and incombustible clothing.
Who would have dared to predict these miracles?

Burgravius has invented the Lamp of Life
which burns brightly if a man is in good health,
grows dim if he's endangered and flickers out
at the moment of death. You may not believe this
but I have a friend whose cousin witnessed it
as well as many another marvel. On the other hand
Burgravius insists diseases can be transmitted
from animals to men by drawing one's blood
and giving it to the other, which is ridiculous.

I've heard of a people called Vishu
who live in a country three months' journey
beyond the land of the Bulgars where every night
is one hour long, and enormous fish in the sea
have tusks which these people take and carve into knives
and sword hilts. And a ship sailing toward the pole
comes to a region where night is unknown
and the sun spins in the firmament like a mill!
Swallow such stories if you like. Myself,
I've been deceived too often.

I've been told Chinese artists may depict nakedness
or coition, but never a female foot.

I've heard the Babylonians had no doctors
and displayed their invalids in the marketplace.
I hardly know what to credit.

They say a certain pharmacist in Germany
gathers queer plants that grow around his village
and distills them in a silver limbeck
for medicinal purposes. I think this is possible.

Chamomile, some claim, is a plant which grows best
when stepped upon. This is plausible.

Antevorta presides over childbirth; postvorta
reminds us of things past. Perhaps.

Granatus, which is a precious stone
like a kernel of pomegranate,
similar to a ruby, comes from Calicut;
hung about the neck or swallowed
it moderates sorrow and revivifies the heart.
Well, I have my doubts.

Any mention of the heart leads us to women.
You should know that the etymology of *femina*
is *fe-mina*—lacking in faith.

The moon's strange power over women is recognized;
so is the fact that idle women are lascivious,
while those with black eyes and shrill voices
are jealous. Seeds in the wind are less fickle.

Like the Anemone, Woman flowers
for a single month.

She's like Cantharides, the Spanish fly
whose golden wings are attached to a poisonous body.

Like the sea, her affections
ebb and flow. What's half so turbulent
as a litigious wife?

Listen. As much difference will be found between women
as between fires. Would you leave the warmth of one
for another?

It's said they shackle our hearts with words
just as we bind a bull's horns with rope.
Indeed, wasn't it Cleopatra's voice
which enamored Antony? The same for Solyman
as he listened to Roxalana.

Wild horses brought to trample Sinalda
refused, and stood away from her in admiration.
Men are equally intimidated.

Alexander, to please his concubine Thais,
set Persepolis afire; Pithidice
for love of Achilles betrayed her island.
Tell me, how and where does love end?

A lovesick Thessalian whose name I don't remember
bit off his thumb to see if his rival would dare as much.
Hunger is easier to endure than love.

Heliogabalus welcomed love
at every orifice of his body.

Hostius constructed a looking-glass
to magnify his virility
while he acted both roles.
Yet not only men do these things:
women go with goats, horses
and swine, which explains Minotaurs,
Sphinxes, Sylvanuses, Centaurs
and other abominations.

Love manifests itself everywhere,
even to inanimate beings.
How does the lodestone draw iron
if not by love?
Why does the earth covet rain?

Saint Jerome thinks every creature loves something,
and nothing has been discovered that does not
—down to the very rocks.

Did you know that trees are not immune?
If the wind brings another's smell to them
they are deeply affected and sometimes marry.
At Brundusium there was a male palm tree,
and a female at Otranto, and both were barren
until they had grown enough to see each other.

Birds are much affected. They sing for joy, yes,
but also in the hope of venery.

Fishes, as you know, become lean and rampant
if they're denied.

Listen. There was a swan at Windsor
that learned of another cock beside his mate
and swam many miles to catch up to it and kill it
and next returned to kill his own hen.

Some creatures are more jealous than swans.
Hieroglyphics describe the venereal passion
of camels which are so jealous they expect the worst
and prefer solitude to enjoy their sensual pleasures
alone. Crocodiles, I hear, are almost the same;
but human jealousy exceeds everything. Bald men,
especially, are suspicious.

Saxo Grammaticus speaks of a bear that loved a woman
so much he kept her in his den for several years
and had a son by her who fathered the Northern Kings.
If this sounds implausible, think about the dolphin
that loved a boy and swam ashore after his death
and so itself perished.

There was a crane in Majorca that loved a Spaniard
and enjoyed walking beside him along the beach,
and would search for him while he was out visiting
and make a loud noise and knock at his door.
And at last after the Spaniard had gone away
the crane stopped eating and died. On the island
they'll tell you that without love we are finished.

There was a woman who ground up her dead husband's bones
for a broth which she drank, in order to have him buried
within herself.

Gismunda ate her lover's heart.
Isn't love a fearsome business?

Petrarch, by the Pope's intervention,
was offered Laura,
but prudently rejected her.

Empedocles was present when the body of a youth
who had died mysteriously was being cut up;
they found his lungs dry and his liver smoky,
his heart scorched from the vehemence of love.

A Roman author mentions a handsome youth who fornicated
with two women in a single night. One wished to marry him,
the other wanted to see him hang. Tell me, if you know:
which came first, which second?

A courtier who had been ordered by King Seleucus
to escort the Queen to Syria cut off his own genitals
and left them in the palace in a wooden box,
for fear he might be accused of lying with her.
And as he suspected, she began to love him;
and when he refused to embrace her she was furious
and later denounced him to the King. But he saved himself
by opening the box to display his mouldering flesh.

Saint Francis, who confessed women in private,
stripped himself naked before the Bishop of Assisi
to prove he was gelded. There are many such men,
God knows.

The inhabitants of Sestos after Leander's death
consecrated Hero's lantern to Anteros, and proclaimed
that whoever was successful in love should light it.
As expected, nobody came forward.

Are women less unfortunate? According to travelers
in Italy where families consist of several daughters
the attractive ones get married; but if they are ugly
their names are changed to Dorothy, Ursula, or Bridget
and they are hidden in monasteries.

A young Greek traveling from Cenchreae to Corinth
met a beautiful woman who took him by the hand

and led him home, saying she was by birth Phoenician
and if he would stay with her a little while
she would play and sing for his entertainment
and pour his wine. He agreed to this, and presently
thought he would marry her. But to their wedding
came Apollonius who learned that she was a serpent
—a Lamia whose furniture was like Tantalus' gold.
Seeing herself revealed, she begged Apollonius
to be silent. When he swore he wouldn't—well,
they say the house and plate and everything else
vanished in an instant. Maybe you laugh at the story.
I don't.

Here's another. This happened in the year 1058.
A young Roman who'd recently gotten married
was out walking with one of his friends
when they came to a tennis court in the fields.
For safekeeping, the bridegroom took off his ring
and put it on the finger of a statue of Venus
while he and his friend amused themselves.
After the game when he tried to retrieve it
he found that the statue had bent her finger.
He decided to come back for it the next day,
and went home, ate supper and got into bed
with his wife; but during the night the goddess
insinuated herself between them and claimed
he had betrothed himself to her—clasping him
in her bronze arms. The historian Florilegus
thinks the young man was freed by Saturn
who ordered Venus to let him go. I doubt this
as much as I doubt the beginning. However
I do believe the part about her interference.
Even today lovers all too often have difficulty.

The hunger of women for love is not just immoderate
but insatiable. It's different with men. Osmodeus
the demon of lust takes possession of male bodies,
yet when his passion is assuaged he discards them
like bundles of rags. In other words, while a woman
may seem very pleasant to a man at first, at last
there's something oppressive in her presence. And men

from Marcus Aurelius to Solomon have testified to this.
After the first moment of delight what we once wanted
is at best tedious. Who's ever heard a fat bird sing
or known a fat dog to hunt?

Men continually participate in the spirit of the women
whose milk first nourished them, which explains Cato
insisting that his wife suckle the servant children.
It explains Tiberius, whose nurse commonly was drunk;
and Caligula, whose nurse dipped her tits in blood.
Cato, incidentally, was the brother of Servilia
who was Julius Caesar's mistress, and Caesar by her
was Brutus' father—which is why after he was stabbed
he cried out: *Kai su ei ekeinon, kai su teknon?*
That is: Thou art one of them, thou, my son?

Now, getting back to our subject. The strange imaginings
of women work powerfully not just upon their infants
but upon themselves. For instance, there was in Mantua
an euphoniously named women—Elionora Meliorina
who thought she was married to a king, and sometimes
knelt to speak with him. And once, finding a bit of glass
in the street, insisted it was a jewel he had sent her.

A man should pick a wife whose brain is unencumbered
by such infirmities as lachryma, qualms and melancholia.
This last is serious. The word comes from *melaina*—black,
together with *chole* or choler, and might be a disease
or nothing but its symptom—we can't be positive,
although numerous doctors have written definitions.
In any event, it manifests itself as a perpetual
anguish of the soul fastened on a single object,
and in women who are misaffected it can be violent.
The old Egyptians accurately showed it as a hare
seated in her form, which means it's been recognized
for ages, and like most problems bedeviling humanity
only seems unique.

Nobody can count the variety or number of our illnesses.
Pliny estimates them at 300—commencing at the sole,
ascending to the crown.

Christians are known to be debilitated and leprous,
scabby, raving, pocked evilly with white spots,
facial blotches and contagious pestilences.
Jews charge this to their habit of sublunary coupling
before the month's impurities have been disgorged,
and call Christians bloody in their pledges.

Bohemians and Hungarians are subject to lycanthropia.
The unfortunate people stricken by this disease
have hollow eyes and scrofulous legs. In the daytime
they lie concealed, but at night creep abroad
barking and howling, surreptitiously visiting graves,
deserts, hollows and other places normally shunned.
Avicenna thinks lycanthropia occurs most often
during February. A famous lawyer died of it
and there have been two exquisite books on the topic
by an erudite Italian. Beyond these few facts
we know almost nothing; we can only speculate.

I want to be honest. If I deceive you, my friend,
it's not out of malice but from bottomless ignorance.
We see through a glass darkly: *Videmus nunc, etc.*

The chief organ of our upper parts, of course,
is the Brain, which is soft, marrowish and whitish
and sits regally by itself within the skull.
Not only is it the Soul's dwelling-house
but the habitation of clemency, grace, reason,
memory and judgment, where a man is most like God.

The Heart is the seat and fountain of life,
of heat, of spirits, of pulse and respiration.
It is the body's sun, the king that rules it,
the organ of each passion and affection.
Pyramidical in form, it is like a pineapple
able to dilate or contract. Of our parts
this organ comes to life first and dies last.

Probably the Soul lasts until the body putrefies
and resolves itself into its primary substance,
at which time it is extinguished and vanishes.

But until then, while the body is being consumed
the Soul wanders about, observing and suffering.

To the best of my knowledge these things are true,
although I claim neither omniscience nor quasi-divinity.
As Horace wrote, we're dust and shadow. *Pulvis et umbra*
sumus.

I narrate these remarks for the benefit of my new wife
who's hardly more than a child. She listens attentively,
or pretends to, while she brushes her hair. What I'd do
if she left me, I have no idea. She's my greatest help.
Without her considerate audience, in spite of my age
I would begin to doubt myself. Any man who does this
is useless.

Adam begat of his first wife Lilith nothing except devils;
I did the same. What became of her and of our six children
I don't know. I care even less.

A devil, by the way, is a slender incomprehensible
spirit that winds itself into bodies where it crouches
among the bowels vitiating health and shaking the mind
with hideous furies. Flies in summer aren't as numerous
as these messengers of Evil. On the 20th of June, 1484,
at Hamel in Saxony a devil disguised as a piper
carried off 130 children.

Water devils cause inundations and shipwrecks
and deceive us in various ways,
choosing frequently to appear in female shape.

Devils which counterfeit suns or moons
or perch on ship's masts, we call Dioscuri.

Devils bedeck themselves with myriad hues and colors,
blend into noises and approximate all imaginable odors.
Blazing stars and *ignes fatui* or firedrakes
are their handiwork leading us toward precipices.
Miraculous alterations in air are their production,

and wonderful effects. They know how to conquer armies.
They help, injure, further, cross and blight
almost all of our projects. Charles the Great
wanted to construct a channel between the Danube
and the Rhine, but what his workmen accomplished by day
was destroyed at night—which gives you some idea
of their capabilities. It would be foolish, however,
to accept the common notion that they penetrate the heart
in order to unlock its deepest mysteries. In any event
you may save yourself by pronouncing the name of God
with a clear voice: *Eloïm, Essaïm, frigativi at appellav* ...

Have I been asleep or awake?
Images flash on the drowsy mind.
Bright wings rise and whirl.
Meteors whisper greenly overhead.
The luminous earth enlarges and diminishes,
enlarges and diminishes, creating and destroying
unknown constellations. *Pater noster,*
qui es ...

Copernicus speaks of infinite spaces
and immense suns, which is horrifying.
We like to think the Cosmos is moderate
and comfortable, familiar as the Bible
represents it. If astronomers were correct
how could we feel at ease?

The sun is exactly 32 miles in width,
situated 3,000 miles from the earth.
This is because God created the sun
to provide illumination for us,
which means it must be near the subjects
for which it was intended. Tell me,
would you build yourself a house in Zion
but set the lamp in Massachusetts?

No human beings can live opposite us
on the underside of the world. If they did
how would they see Christ descend from Heaven
at the Second Coming?

Don't listen to false prophets. When they talk to you
about improbabilities, turn deaf ears. Believe me,
the principle behind the domestic electric light
is scarcely worth the attention of practical men,
and suffocation lies in wait for speeding travelers.

No conceivable arrangement of substances, apparatus
and energy could possibly be united to build a device
by which men might fly long distances through the air,
because resistance increases as the square of the speed
and the work as the cube. Mark my words. The concept
of gigantic machines wafting innumerable passengers
across oceans and deserts is a secular delusion.

Fridtjof Nansen has located the North Pole,
which is the apex of scientific accomplishment;
no future discoveries of much consequence
should be anticipated.

Confine yourself to categorical realities,
my friend. Man attached to himself takes error
for truth, lies for verities. Imagine it like this:
ancient Egyptians in the arrogance of their achievement
constructed monuments that outlived their civilization.
A word to the wise is sufficient.

Humanus oculus non videt.

When Satan plummeted from Heaven
and emerald dropped out of his crown,
and from it the Holy Grail was fashioned.

The Ten Commandments were first inscribed on a sapphire

Bishops wear sapphire rings. But do you know why?
Because this stone preserves chastity and wards off Evil.
Mirabilia testimonia tue, Domine. Lord, thy marvels
be thy witness.

Look. Two tremendous rocks circle the planet Mars.
The inner satellite, Phobos, completes a revolution

in 7½ hours; the larger, Deimos, requires 36 hours.
Both are too small to be accurately measured,
even their existence was not confirmed until 1877;
yet 151 years earlier Jonathan Swift had described
an extraordinary flying island known as Laputa
whose astronomers find two satellites circling Mars
in 10 and 20 hours. Skeptics call this coincidence,
others say it demonstrates suprahuman comprehension.

And what of Flaubert's ominous precognition?
He foresaw an age toward which the world was bending
—an era of utilitarianism, militarism
and the steep rise of America.

When asked to compare America with a previous nation
Arnold Toynbee replied that it corresponds to Rome
under Cicero during the final days of the Republic
because of the inconceivable power it employs
to the distress and suffering of so many people,
because of a Constitution which once was admirable
but is now invalid, because of disorder at home
and, above all else, because of violence.
Plague creeps down our doors;
a foul odor spreads.

Oremus.

My neighbor, a dramatist,
sees us as curiously Sophoclean
in our tragedy—presenting us to ourselves
at the moment of perceiving our guilt.

Remember, a fragile membrane divides the past
and the present. Germans on trial at Nuremberg
explained that certain regrettable situations
developed because of the Jews themselves:
if, instead of clawing and struggling
in an obviously futile attempt to survive,
they had calmly obeyed instructions
they would have suffered very little.

Solibor: 250,000.

Chelmo. Treblinka. Belzec. Sachsenhausen.
Is it time to forget? Already these places
have lost meaning, and tomorrow—well,
my friend, King Assurbanipal of Nineveh
enjoyed dining in the garden with his wife
while the severed heads of defeated monarchs
dangled from nearby trees. A bit repugnant,
otherwise who cares?

What matters to me and my wife is that our son
was killed. We got a notice from Washington
saying he died valiantly for a noble cause
someplace in Asia. I think it comforted my wife,
but as for me—I guess I've already told you
I remember too much.

Certain grievances can't be arbitrated.
Cardinal Cresence died at Verona
thinking a black dog had followed him
to his deathbed, which no man could drive off.
What lay on this man's conscience?
And will those responsible for my son
one day hear the sound of a black dog trotting?

Embittered royalists in Revolutionary times
spelled out TP—for Thomas Paine—with nails
on the soles of their shoes so that at every step
they could trample his spirit. I've done the same
to curse a leader whose name is anathema.

Let me teach you Carducci's hymn to Satan:
I inspire the revolter, the scorner, the skeptic,
the satirist. I still distribute the Tree of Knowledge.
I am the soul of the world. I am the lightning
of the human mind. I level thrones and altars,
annihilate blinding cust . . .

Look. Sultan Baibars died after accidentally
drinking from a poisoned cup he had prepared
for somebody else, which was appropriate.
Now we wait to register Johnson's death.
We are mad not just individually but nationally,
Seneca tells us: we punish isolated murder,
yet what of war which murders thousands?

Well, the wider the scope of my reflections
the more obviously they mock every human plan.
Because of this I note in my journal not only Evil
itself, but those who do Evil—thus perpetuating
particular names for the reprobation of posterity.

If what I write troubles you, remember my name:
Dom Helder Camara, Archbishop of Recife,
whose vocation is to argue, argue, argue, argue
for moral pressure against the lords.

Look. The Pentagon contracts with 48 universities
to assess the potential usefulness of birds
in aerial photography, land mine detection, gunnery
and the direction of missiles. The air itself
turns alien and weird.

Circles narrow; days shorten.
Fitfully the President washes his hands.

Telephones in every agency are suspect,
and all conference rooms.
Mirrors open.

Yesterday a police car followed my nephew
because he had been distributing pamphlets.
The car stopped, three officers got out.
After questioning my nephew they handcuffed him
and, as the saying goes, took him into custody.
I've done nothing about it, nor do I intend to.
I won't even attempt to communicate with him.
More accurately than he, I read the hour.

Listen, my friend. In the Nazi camps it was forbidden
to rescue a man who wanted to hang himself. *Was du erlebt,*
kann keine Macht der Welt dir rauben.

I can't predict the ultimate result of surveillance,
however a couple of remarks might be relevant. First,
early in American history anybody caught eating mince pie
was suspected of royalist sympathies. Second, the historian
Tacitus mentioned the Crucifixion while failing utterly
to apprehend its significance. In other words, our eyes
focus best on what they're accustomed to seeing.

Do you own records by Paul Robeson? Drawings
or paintings by Pablo Picasso? Henri Matisse?
Are you now, or have you at any time in the past
studied the Russian language?

Ah, but who's to guard the guards?
Juvenal asks: *Quis custodiet ipsos custodes?*

I hear the ring of an axe against wood
and wait for signs of disaster on the wind.
Listen: on the 16th of February, 1568,
every inhabitant of the Netherlands
was condemned to death for heresy. *Ora pr . . .*

King Charles, petitioned by the citizens of Granada
to control the Holy Inquisition, refused to intervene,
citing the irrevocable separation of Church and State.

Powers accumulate. American police disguise themselves
as Catholic priests, which speaks for itself.

Midday. In the oppressive silence
wandering uneasily from one room to the next
I lose myself like a wretched Greek among the corridors
of Knossos. *En nukti boule tois sophois gignetai.*

Midnight. I'm the philosopher Callisthenes
who could find no subject worthy of his pen;

the soldier Chamus who wounded King Cyrus
and went mad with arrogance; Pythagoras
who thought he could read what was written
on the moon.

I become Pasetes the juggler, whose magic obolus
returned to his purse whenever he spent it.

I? Who am I? Vatinius
ridiculing his own deformed feet;
the poet Sigüenza y Góngora
arguing against comets;
Lully transmuting lead into gold;
Kepler adhering to a notion of infinity
as the second focus of a parabola
while reason assured him it was absurd;
Saint Margaret Marie Alacoque
searching for dusty bread;
Newton evolving a system in solitude
during the plague;
Ibn Jaqub on his endless journey
across fields and through vast palaces
of memory. Yet I am Paracelsus
above all.

*I am what is
and is not.*

Hmm. Ah-hemm! My friend the scholar defines
Transcendentalism as the spiritual cognoscence
of psychological irrefragability
associated with concutient ademption
of incolumnient spirituality and etherialized
contention of subsultory concretion.
I would be interested to know if you agree.

Let me pause long enough to say that in Cromwell's time
the practice of hemming or coughing ornamentally
became fashionable, and when sermons were published
each spot where the preacher hemmed or coughed was noted
in the margin. I thought perhaps you'd wondered.

Now, suppose we continue. On the subject of false logic
Peter Roget remarks that too often disguised
under specious phraseology it gains the assent
of unthinking multitudes, disseminating black seeds
of prejudice and perpetuating error: therefore
it is of great consequence that strict accuracy prevail
and regulate our use of language.

Needless to say, it is through the marvelous
and constant use of words that we embody abstractions,
enabling us to glide from premise to conclusion
with such rapidity that the mind, like a child,
holds little memory of successive steps.

I have somewhere read, or a friend once told me,
that each workman for the exercise of his art
must be provided with appropriate implements
—tools for the artisan, costumes for the actor,
colors, pens, canvas and brushes for the painter.
So it is with metaphysicians and philosophers,
who require the instrumentality of words. Words
and words: with them we encompass our thought,
identify prehensile filaments of association,
exemplify feeling, or show that felicitous diction
needed for graceful and persuasive eloquence.
Such abilities may not be demanded very often,
yet we do miss them if they're neglected.

I have been thinking about Maurice Goguel,
for fifty years a professor at the *Faculté Libre
de Théologie Protestante* of the Univserity of Paris,
who concentrated his entire intellectual life
and all of his efforts on one century and a half
of Christian history. *Jésus et les origines
du Christianisme* is his masterpiece, whose narrowness,
austerity of style, and reluctance to please
insure its universal unpopularity. As a result
there are those who claim Goguel wasted his life.
Others argue. Myself, I consider it a serious problem
knotted with pedantry, dedication and high competence.

The same might be said of a German scholar, one Ginzel
early in this century who published a three-volume
Handbuch der mathematischen und technischen Chronologie
which includes the dates of new moons over Babylon
—but no subject has been more thoroughly researched
than that remorseless deity who inspired Maurice Goguel.

Dionysius Exiguus, a Greek monk living in Rome
during the 6th century, calculated that Jesus was born
in 754 *ab urbe condita*. That is, in the first year
of the 195th Olympiad—an interesting deduction.
However, our best information comes from the Gospels.
If Matthew correctly dates the flight into Egypt
Jesus must have been born during the final year
of the reign of King Herod, who died in 4 B.C.
Yet if we choose to accept the chronology of Luke,
who clearly associates the nativity with a census,
we discover that the date must be 6 or 7.
In neither instance can we call 1 A.D. acceptable.
Be this as it may, we do not care very much
about such scholarship, no matter how convincing,
unless it seems both particular and universal,
somehow indicating the nature of a moralist.
For this I find myself obligated to Thucydides,
who distinguished the essential from the casual.

To Edward Gibbon I am indebted for pointing out
that the inhabitants of a declining empire
could be lured into military service only by dread
of punishment or hope of profit, however miserable.
Obvious parallels present themselves.

During the second half of the fourth century
an anonymous pamphlet addressed to an emperor,
probably Valentinian the First, offered proposals
toward reform of the army, savagely attacked
the cost of the perpetual warfare of those times,
oppressive taxation, and the corrupt and extortionate
provincial administration of the Roman empire.
Whether or not Valentinian saw this pamphlet

we do not know; we do know that his attitude
remained imperial. Tell me, when have Kings,
Presidents and Emperors listened to distant voices
before the crest of violence smashed chancellery windows?

In his *Consilium Aegyptiacum* the philosopher
Leibniz suggested to King Louis Quatorze
that France undertake the colonization of Egypt
as a link with the opulent lands of the Orient.
Instead, Louis decided to attack the Low Countries
—a scheme as stupidly brutal and useless
as any that sucked the brain of Johnson or Nixon.

Socrates, incidentally, disapproved of the democratic concept
of popular elections. If we reflect that Congress allocates
$23,000 annually for the purchase of paintings and sculpture
and $78,000,000,000 for weapons—well, in France they say
Chacun à son goût.

Some think the evil of a so-called "free society"
is epitomized by the trial and execution of Socrates
who, in contrast to the rhetorical brilliance of Miletus,
argued ineptly, reminding us of the physicist Oppenheimer
brought to trial by a degenerate Senator named McCarthy
and convicted by a nation desperately resisting logic.

Is democracy, as many people claim,
a sinister form of misrule?

Of political perversions, is tyranny the worst
and democracy the best? The first elevates the tyrant,
the second debases the people.

It's worth noting that Moctezuma was elected
not because of any great accomplishment
nor because he was intelligent,
but because he so meticulously respected
traditional Aztec ritual and ceremony.
Does this sound familiar?

I have one additional comment. The ancient Incas
recognized a difference between robbery from malice
and robbery from want. In the latter instance
some official was punished instead of the thief,
for lack of adequate administration. Wisely, I think,
we don't compare primitive attitudes with our own.

3:20 P.M. My spine hurts.
I fold myself like a nut
to fight the pain.
I feel myself swimming
dizzily in widening circles. *De l'audace,*
encore de l'audace, touj . . .

My stepfather can't understand what I'm doing.
I point out to him those strangely delicate traceries
autumn rain makes down the glass. I point to them and wait.
He just shakes his head.

A note from my wife. She's gone to the polls.
She complains because I criticize but won't vote.
I content myself with rereading Plato's 7th letter
in which he speaks of his disgust with public affairs
and of how he'd expected to take part in government
until he saw the level of corruption. Then as now
one hand washes the other.

Corruption, murder, theft—name what you like.
However reprehensible, these don't seem puzzling;
but I admit I'm staggered by pious ignorance.
According to Governor Bickett of North Carolina
military conscription was divinely ordained:
Of course there are some differences in details
but the principle of the selective service law
is identical with the draft law given to Moses
by Jehovah in the Wilderness of Sinai.

Next, may I introduce Senator Russell from Georgia:
If we have to start over again with another
Adam and Eve, I want them to be Americans.
I want them on this continent and not in Europe.

Just as instructive is the Honorable Carl Durham
objecting to a cartoon of Adam and Eve
in United States Public Affairs Pamphlet No. 85
because both figures have been depicted with navels,
which Congressman Durham cites as unmistakable evidence
of the subversive influence of atheistic Communism.

Now if you think times change, my friend,
let me point out that every morning
the Senate doors swing shut
after a traditional prayer. *Pater nost*...

In June of 1775 a resolution was passed by the Congress
disclaiming any intent to invade Canada. A month later
an invasion was secretly authorized. In April of 1970
we were assured by Secretary Rogers that no Americans
would be sent into Cambodia. Within 5 days what happened?

Will our last liberty be the option to believe or disbelieve?

There are those who think we prepare a vial of rage
for ourselves to drink; vengeance is being stored.

Lethal biological agents have been tested in Malaysia,
England, Sweden, Cyprus, Alaska, Ireland, Germany,
Greenland, Australia, Taiwan and God knows where else.

Government scientists, unable to destroy what they concocted,
created a poisoned lake 2 miles deep in the earth
beneath the city of Denver.

Military equipment costing 25 million dollars
was authorized for a clique of Greek colonels
—an amount considered insufficient by the Pentagon
which privately donated 26 million dollars more.
A spokesman explained: *Gentlem*...

Look. We've sown bombs like seeds across the Orient.
Would you care to predict the harvest?

Look. Relocation Centers are being planned
for those adjudged inimical to National Security.

Ora pro nobis.

Having devastated a Thai village by mistake
the U.S. Air Force proffered compensation
in the form of a detonating apparatus
which the villagers hauled away on a cart
and sold to a scrap metal dealer for $30.
Can you isolate this mad episode's madness?

Or this: a U.S. sergeant, Esequiel Torres,
rode triumphantly through Brownsville, Texas,
hailed by members of the local American Legion
after being accused of murdering civilians.
Goya, we know, was obsessed by similar scenes;
we know, too, how quickly the populace forgets.

Problems as old as the black snow of Anaxagoras
sift toward us; few, if any, can be resolved.
Why bother to embalm the malady of a continent,
measure the length of Achilles' whiskers,
count the number of knots on Hercules' club?
Why trouble ourselves with negative commandments?

I stopped a senile priest at his rounds,
one eye shut, the other dull in the lamplight
—the ball of it hard, opaque, yellow as a lump
of frozen marrow protruding from his skull.
Father, I said, will you explain everything?
He nodded and blessed me and told me the names
of nine men celebrated during the Middle Ages:
Hector, Alexander, Caesar, Joshua, David, Judas
Maccabeus, King Arthur, Charlemagne and Godfrey
of Bouillon. Three of them were Gentiles, three
Hebrews, three Christians. *Mirabilia testimonia
tue, Domine.*

Father, I said, does the Crusade fulfill a wish
deeply rooted in the Western mind?

The blood of our enemy is pleasant to God,
he said, and the blood of the faithful also
because it is the blood of martyrs.

Father, I said, I remember helicopters arriving
at dusk, leaflets fluttering on the rice paddies
and Colonel Giteau watching through binoculars.
I saw the dragon ships fly over and flares drop
in rings around native huts. The military legion, anchor
and trumpet were invented by Etruscans, he said.

Father, I said, we could hear the people inside.
When I was a kid in Ohio a stable caught fire
and the horses screamed like that. Expeditions
to the North Pole may prove beneficial to the soul,
he said.

Father, I said, shouldn't all of us work incessantly
to undermine the system of armed alliances?
If not, how are we the instruments of His peace?
Conquistadors were mistaken for angels, he said.

Father, I said, because God is immense
and infinite and His nature imperfectly known
shouldn't He be worshipped diversely?
Unorthodox convictions, my son, he replied,
suggest heresy. Thank you, Father, I said.
He blessed me again and I continued on my way.

Clarior ex obscuro.

As you see, I eschew succinct interpretations;
I obey each intuition and decide nothing in advance.
I set down thoughts that I'm unable to understand;
I proceed without volition, mindless as a spider
spinning patterns from the substance of its entrails.
At times I'm sustained by the nuances of my voice,
at other times simply by leaving a little of myself
in a moist crevice of my wife's body.

When I was young I abstained from women,
but there comes a time when our best intents
lie subservient to the body's obligation.
Ever the river Alpheus, I'm told, was unable
to avoid contemplating Arethusa.

Take a look at the Cretan frescoes. Notice
with what indifference Minoan men were drawn
but with what care, obvious love and regard for detail
the women have been delineated.

Toltec Indians many centuries ago painted a garden
in which there was a snake coiled around a tree
with its head thrust searchingly through the foliage,
its face a woman's face. Not much changes.

According to the French, a woman's sword
is her tongue, which never rusts.
La langue des femmes est leur épée, etc.

Arabs compare women to camels, and say they are graceful
hideous creatures with magic in their way of walking.

Myself, I think that whoever takes a woman to his heart
establishes a religion with a fallible goddess.
Having been married 20 years I've observed women
too closely not to fear them. My wife now requests
a correction which she says is important. All right:
30 years. God save us.

My wife's brother is a hunchback whose slow liquid eyes
bulge with desperate stupidity. That, in conjunction
with a stringy mustache, gives him the appearance
of an unsuccessful prawn. His health isn't very good
and he has few interests. If we talk to each other
it's just to be civil. The fact that I travel quite a bit
dumbfounds him. Why did you go to Guatemala? he asked.
I said I had gone to sift through the Mayan ruins
at Tikal in hopes of uncovering some decorated pottery
or, with luck, a jade earplug. At the mention of jade

he blinked, as I thought he might. Avarice, avarice.
Otherwise he scarcely listened; I could see boredom
settle on his face like dust falling in an empty room.
Well, in the kingdom of the blind the one-eyed is king.

Regarding my own appearance, I've sometimes been told
I bear a curious resemblance to Henry the Navigator
—bony equine features with fleshy lips, lusterless gaze.
I've studied his portrait. To me he looks troubled,
perhaps by some gastrointestinal complaint. Distracted
and fretted. Yes, we do look a little alike. I've heard
he ordered his caravels toward the Cape of Good Hope
year after year, trying to join forces with the legendary
Prester John of Ethiopia in order to outflank the Moors
and crush Islam forever. How sad, when all this time
in green neglected hugeness lay another continent.
That might seem irrelevant, but where the heart leads
our feet follow. *Lá vão os pés onde quer o coração.*

Lat. 06.43 s.; Long. 11.21 E.
Five centuries ago Diego Cam
identified the mouth of the Congo
where it empties into the Atlantic.
There he raised an alabaster cross
in perpetual memory of the event
with this inscription:
In the year 6681
of the world
and in 1482 since . . .

People will tell you that the site
where the nails of the Passion were forged
has been finally located, and someone has picked up
the stone that slew Goliath, and recovered the bloody lance
that pierced His side, and the star that guided the Magi
has been retrieved from the depths of an ancient well
in Bethlehem where it was observed to fall
on the day of the Epiphany. I have my doubts.
I'm less credulous, less submissive than I was.

I suggest that nothing exists more pitiable
or presumptuous than Man. I cite as evidence
a shipload of pilgrims returning from Mecca
which was seized and set afire by Christians;
the treaty of Tordesillas whereby Spain
and Portugal agreed to divide the world;
Pizarro—courageous, determined and durable,
who destroyed an empire while contributing nothing;
a Spanish admiral with an impoverished fleet
near the Orinoco who thought he had located
the fabulous river Gihon, and wrote as follows:
There are here great indications suggesting
the proximity of earthly Paradise. Not only
does it correspond in mathematical position
with the opinions of holy and learned theologians,
but all other signs concur to make it probable.

Of course such presumption isn't limited
to Mediterraneans. There was the Pole in 1518
during the reign of King Sigismund who announced
that he was Christ and collected 12 apostles
and judged the world; there was the Englishman
Macaulay writing his *Universal History of Mankind*
at the age of eight; and Al-Mamun who governed
from the Indus to the Andalus, but at the same time
admitted he couldn't control 16 puppets on a table.

P-Q3.
P-Q4.

Now let me mention a conceited prince, Naym Lap,
who landed with a vast flotilla on the Chimu coast
such a long time ago there is no way to speak of it,
who brought not only his consort but many other women,
an army of soldiers together with their followers,
a trumpeter, a cupbearer, a master of ceremonies,
a cook, a tailor, a bath attendant, and another man
whose one duty in life was to paint the prince's face.

Musicians, too, indulge themselves.
Scriabin delivered a sermon to the waves
from a boat on Lake Geneva.

Animals are not exempt:
Incitatus, the horse of Caligula,
ate from an ivory manger,
drank from a golden bucket
and slept in a marble stall.

Has modesty vanished from the world?
Que sçais-je?

What do I know? Let me answer elliptically.
My grandfather gave me a teleidoscope
when I was a child, which I've never lost.
I always carry it on my travels
and pay no attention to people who stare at me
as I examine their quadrilateral features.
You have a single view of Manco Capac, for instance,
but I have several. I'll show you one.
Look, you recognize him as the first Inca
whereas I see him as the son of Kublai Khan
who conquered Peru with a brigade of elephants.

You consider Wat Tyler an insurrectionist;
I see him murdered by the mayor of London.
Now in this context, which hand washes which?

I have studied the counsel of my preceptor
Borges, who thinks enduring wisdom
must be everything to all men,
capable of infinite ambiguity, a mirror
reflecting each—a map of the universe.
I am grateful for the instruction
but I learn best through specifics.

It's late. A dog barks. I turn on the bed,
sick with desire and pointless suffering.
It seems to me I hear the tinkle of camel bells

and the guttural noises of blue-black Senegalese
bringing ivory to market. It was written
in Ecclesiasticus that we should travel
to foreign places and good and evil try
in all things. What deity have I offended?

Be at peace with God, we're told
—whatever we conceive Him to be.
Regardless of one's aspiration
in the grief and confusion of life
let each keep peace with his soul.
Let go of love. Let go of sorrow.

I hear words, but they pass by
like the waters of the Rhine.

Pater nost . . .

Among the rubbish heaps
of an ancient city called Oxyrhynchus
a party of British explorers came upon a leaf
from a papyrus book composed during the second century
on which was written the beginnings of seven sentences,
each introduced by the words "Jesus says."
The rest is gone, but who knows?
Maybe it wasn't especially significant.

Not far from Hebron on the mount of Mamre
stands an oak which the Saracens call *Dirpe*,
and we call the Dry Tree, because it has been there
since the beginning of time and was green
and had leaves until the day Our Lord perished.
If a Western Prince shall sing mass beneath this tree
it will once more turn green and bear leaves,
unless the hour happens to have passed.

Mundus vult decip . . .

If a man casts a ball of iron into the Dead Sea
it will float; but a feather on the Dead Sea goes down
because it represents those who sin.

Close by the Dead Sea grow apples beautiful to behold,
but whoever cuts into them finds them black with cinders
—a token that Almighty God has scorched this land
with his wrath. And the cities of Gomorrah, Sodom,
Zeboim, Aldama and Zoar have sunk beneath a briny lake.

The Gardens of the Hesperides on a mysterious island
overflowing with golden apples somewhere in the ocean
represent everything toward which we direct our lives.
Scandinavians like to speak of a place called Asgard
which they regard as the abode of happiness and bliss;
they say it exists in the heart of a fruitful land
watered by rivers of milk flowing to the cardinal points.
Singhalese know of an everlasting dwelling place,
hill-encompassed, for those who are wise and just,
which they have named Ilà. Buddhists think of Sineru,
a mountain summit upon which holy Tawrrutisa is founded.
Hindus contemplate the radiant center of Jambadwípa
with its soaring golden peak Slávratta, celestial earth,
city of Brahma, out of which gush four primeval rivers
reflecting the colorific glories of their source
—northward, southward, eastward and westward.
Furthermore, the Hebrews have heard of such a place,
called Eden. *Crescite et multiplicamini et repl...*

Tartars, I think, have no knowledge of a celestial city,
nor of any settled city; but the boundaries of their land
are understood, and they know where to feed their cattle
in winter, in autumn, in summer and in spring.

I've just been asked if I, myself, believe in Paradise.
I'll respond intuitively: discoveries break successively
upon the consciousness of travelers and philosophers.

Quite a few years I've spent arguing and meditating,
to say nothing of a thousand places I've visited,
so you can judge for yourself my qualifications.
Pay no attention to my detractors. They complain
that I enter the temple of knowledge backward;
but controversy invigorates us. Isn't this true?

I offer for your examination various leitmotifs,
reveries, hypotheses and proposals, some of which
are my own, others adapted or stolen from masters.
Here's a thought of Anaximander: Stars lie closer to us
than either the moon or the sun, his conviction
predicated on the purity of numbers.
What do you think about that?

Ptolemy's convinced the earth must be globular
because it isn't cylindrical, flat or polyhedral.
Aristotle, too, thinks it must be a globe
but probably overestimates its circumference.
Eratosthenes claims to have determined the radius
of its curvature, and from this obtains a figure
for its circumference which, by his calculations,
must approximate 250,000 stadia—all because
sunlight casts no shadow in a well at Syene
during the summer solstice and because Alexandria
lies on the same meridian. Now, what do you say?
Are these three right about the earth's form?

Let me warn you that the logical necessity
of bodies falling toward the center of a globe
would meet strict theological opposition.

As suspicious of truth as of heresy
the Church is quick to attack Copernicus.
Luther calls him a fool. Melancthon demands
reprisal. *De Revolutionibus Orbium Caelestium*
goes on the Index. Well, how about it?
Is religion an oak with dead roots?

Have you been dismayed by papal rhetoric
on the subject of contraception?
Do stars shine for empty laws of our devising?

Listen, my friend. There was a Jesuit of Ingolstadt
who repeated certain observations until he was positive
that he had discovered spots on the face of the sun.
But when he informed the Provincial Father of the Order

his superior replied that, having consulted authorities
and been unable to find references to such phenomena,
these so-called spots resulted from a defective lens
—either that, or they were defects in the Jesuit's eyes
because the sun is the symbol of incorruptibility
and to demean it would be tantamount to the crime of
lèse-majesté, thus imperiling Christian dogma.

No doubt Christianity remains a source of symbols
for millions—the cravings of their imagination
satisfied by New Testament parables, oil portraits
and revised pagan legends concerning Life, Death
and Resurrection. Nevertheless, its hold on the mind
is weakening. Philosophies shrivel, gods vanish.

Pope Paul VI denounces popular music, comedies
and nudist conventions. *L'Osservatore Romano*,
obedient and immaculate, makes known to us
that at the end of this path we shall find
no values—only corruption on a universal scale.

Pater noster, qui es in coelis: sanctificet . . .

Japanese Christians, stunned by a miraculous cloud,
were seen wandering through the blistered streets
of Hiroshima murmuring: *Shu Jesusu! Shu Jesusu!*
Somewhat later, less mystical Japanese physicists
with Lauritsen electroscopes understood only too well
the full degree of Protestant vengeance. *Shu Jesusu,
awaremi tamai.*

Deaths attributed to leukemia occur more often
at Hiroshima than at Nagasaki. Guess why.
The United States experimented with uranium
on the first city, with plutonium on the next.
Pray for us, if you like. Not that it matters.

The dead press no moral obligations on the living;
that's our obligation. It explains why I call myself
Dom Helder Camara. Don't forget.

Consider the State of New York, whose officials
resolved to find a dignified method of execution.
Having tentatively decided on an electric chair
they bought an orangutan about the size of a man,
tied it to the chair and turned on the current.
The beast's hair caught fire and it began struggling
but before long it was quite satisfactorily charred.
The first human subject was one William Kemmler.
After he had been strapped in place a hemispherical
electrode was fitted to his head and another electrode
attached to his back. The warden then gave a signal.
The executioner pulled a lever and Kemmler jumped.
The voltage was increased but under this load the electrodes
started flickering. Kemmler, meanwhile, had begun to fight
with such fury that the ponderous chair rocked and tilted.
Smoke was seen curling from his flesh and purplish foam
came dribbling through his lips while the executioner
methodically continued lifting and depressing the lever.
When he seemed to be dead the current was turned off,
he was unstrapped, placed on a gurney and wheeled away
to the autopsy room where his clothes were removed.
The examiners found that Kemmler's skin had cracked
like the canvas of a Renaissance painting. His skull
was sawed in half, but they could find no blood,
only an odd black substance resembling charcoal.
His brain had been baked as hard as a stone.
Now don't you find this instructive?

Move a little closer; it's important
that you and I understand each other.
The State is solicitous and humane.
It is, let me assure you. The condemned
must always be in good health,
and before his execution he's fed.
As you know, he's given fresh clothing,
although one thing you may not know:
it's considered good form on his part
to shake hands with the warden
and to thank him for any past favors.

In order that spectators wouldn't be offended
by facial contortions, excretory odors,
torn flesh, gouts of blood or a severed head
the State of California selected gas,
a method of execution highly recommended
by the inimitable Nazis.

Here's something else: King Louis XI of France
thought executions were wasteful unless the death
somehow contributed to the advancement of science,
so every now and then court adjourned to a cemetery
where the King's throne was set beside an open grave
and a prisoner who had been tied to a slab was vivisected
by a surgeon who explained to the attentive monarch
and to his courtiers how the living body functions.
Thus, it was felt, knowledge of medicine increased;
and King Louis was acclaimed for his patronage.

A contract for the construction of the first guillotine
was awarded to a German harpsichord maker, Tobias Schmidt,
who was the low bidder, who explained that periodically
he set aside the practice of his art in order to assist
the realization of discoveries that would benefit humanity.

Speaking of public benefactors, the English poet Southey
struck Napoleon with an axe, dragged him into a hall
and publicly beheaded him. This took place, of course,
in Southey's dream; yet public-minded citizens
are known to contrive improbable, desperate dreams
while the rest of us are taken wholly with ourselves.

Bismarck, meditating on the continuance of national unity,
fell asleep and dreamt he had been given a map of Germany
which grew rotten and crumbled between his fingers.

John Wesley saw himself walking the streets of Bristol
and espied someone he knew, and went across to shake hands
but was unable to do so because his arms were missing.
He soon guessed what this meant: his work was finished
and his intercourse with mortals was about to cease.

Bacon saw his father's house plastered with black mortar
while, unknown to him, his father was dying in London.

William II of England felt a cold wind pass through his side;
the next day Tyrrell's arrow killed him.

Astyagas, the King of Media, saw a vine growing
out of his daughter's womb which spread across Asia;
so when she became pregnant he set a guard over her
to murder the child and circumvent the usurpation
of his empire. But Mandane gave birth to Cyrus,
proving that dreams don't lie, though dreamers do.

Once my sister saw herself holding a book
which she knew was the most precious book extant
because it was composed before the world began.
She remembers that it was not difficult to read
despite a great many scholarly notes, and letters
that seemed strangely small. But as to what it said
—she's forgotten. Maybe you can interpret this,
I can't. I know only that we dream of our desires
with the urgency of sleeping dogs which tremble
and whine and slaver.

Myself, I dream ordinarily of extravagant things
—chimeras and such. Sometimes I relive my youth.
I'm twenty-three, walking on the beach at Málaga
with a little Slavic ballerina whose language
is melodious, if incomprehensible. Or I'm a cadet
dressed in my school uniform. I'm twelve,
quarreling senselessly with my sister.
Years sink beneath the rim of time.

Avant que de désirer fortement
une chose, il faut examiner
quel est le bonheur
de celui qui . . .

I find myself on the rue St. André des Arts
in Paris, eating supper at a Vietnamese restaurant.

Steaming yellow rice with pork, langoustine,
a bottle of Muscadet, white porcelain, bananas
and apples and chopsticks. And a Eurasian girl
with gentle black eyes at a nearby table.
I wonder if it would have been wise to speak:
Bonsoir, Mademoiselle. Bonsoir, Monsieur.
It would have been simple, yes. But I didn't
because of La Rochefoucauld's maxim. Before desiring
a thing passionately one ought always to inquire
into the happiness of him that already possesses it.

Life being as alarming as it is, I prefer the past.
For instance, Madrid is filled with alluring ladies
yet I ignore them. I spend my time in a small gallery
of the Prado where I'm free to speculate and to stare
at Reymerswaele's portrait of a moneylender's wife
motionlessly helping her husband through the centuries.

In Amsterdam I pay my respects to Anna Codde.
I admit to feeling thwarted by the accidental
separation of some four hundred years. I suspect
we might have gone well together. I like her clothes
—puffed sleeves, stylish bodice, pristine cap,
and I think I know what's on this woman's mind,
judging from her indulgent smile. So did Heemskerck,
I'd guess. He probably kept a few sketches.

Greuze's beloved, Mademoiselle Balbuti,
materializes in each of his paintings;
even the portrait of Nap . . .

Uncle just now opened the door to ask what I'm up to.
I live in holes and corners, he thinks, where sunlight
seldom penetrates. He refers to me as a noctambulist
obsessed by foul imaginings, exposing myself through dreams.
Well, his life's a meager draught—dancing, card playing,
repetitiously earning and spending money. I overlook him
and continue to regard human activities not with pleasure
quite so much as with interest.

If I were to characterize myself I would liken myself
to the Florentine painter Benozzo di Lese Gozzoli
who understood very well how to convey the warmth
of a human face, but in drawing his own features
resisted the natural temptation to look attractive.

My temperament is Oriental. Vague descriptions
infatuate me, I become enamored of shadows.
More than the woman I cherish her footprint,
and the use of clysters seems unpleasant
when a sturdy penis serves well enough
to massage or to stimulate the rectum.
You might say I emulate the great conquerors
Bonaparte, Caesar, Alexander and Saladin
who delighted themselves not only as husbands
but as wives. *Trahit sua quemque voluptas.*

Until the creation of Eve
Adam fondled beasts,
Talmudic scholars tell us.

For the sake of the belly
countless roles are played.

Tonight I plan to decorate my scrotum
to attract and fascinate my wife. Why not?

It's useless to struggle against Fate
because no man can reject
what's written on his forehead,
yet wise men know how Nature behaves.
Only a fool accepts Fortune.

I've been told that the Vishnu-bhukteh sect
paint the emblem *naumum* on their foreheads
to symbolize the ripe vulva of a menstruous woman.

The yawning labia of productive women are represented
by the bloom of a lotus, just as its bud symbolizes
a virgin cunnus and its pistil typifies the fetus.
Altogether, this flower is taken to mean the womb.

Seashells, beans and peaches, I have heard
are adored as effigies of the female pudenda.

Datura causes men to grow lustful and exuberant.

Nymphomania is caused by yellowish worms
within, generated by the powerful strokes of Negroes
or of domiciled baboons.

I believe, although I cannot verify it,
that Moslems consider *rejem*, death by lapidation,
a suitable punishment for incest.
I think the golden crescent of El-Islam
means *hheshoom*—the vulva
from the mons veneris as far as the anus,
and the sycamore fig *gemeez* calls to mind
a virgin uterus.

Churreyl, I know, indicates the succubus
and *yukshee* the ravenous nymph.

It's common knowledge that the shame of a man
extends from his navel to his knees;
that of a woman from the peak of her head to her toes.
So be it. Hindus say we shall meet a white crow
or find the imprint of fishes' feet
before we learn what lies in a woman's heart.

I've set down these things for your instruction
because I know that the earth with its many facts,
wonders and immensities, as well as the adventures
which befall pilgrims passing through it,
are astonishing and greatly worth narrating.

Now, come closer. Sit next to me.
What would you like to hear?
I deal mostly in mysteries and fables.
Sometimes I pull teeth for a living,
peddle drugs, market fortunes by the stars,
beg, amuse myself with burghers, copulate

with their maids every chance I get.
After all, the universe is indifferent.
Six years ago I exchanged my painted hat
for the velvet cap and yellow scarf
of a traveling student and since then
have gone from school to school
hungrily seeking knowledge,
but nowhere have I been able to find it.
I stayed at the village of Ingolstadt
and was frustrated by dogmatic lessons.
At Cologne I found obscurantism.
Academies are excellent for training poodles
but that's not what I want. In short,
necessity obliges me to travel. Come along
or stay put. Suit yourself.

Pilgrims returning from the Crusades
speak of the marvelous sidicus bird
which is green over its entire body
except for the feet and the beak
and a band encircling the neck,
all of which are red, and a long tail
—oh, a prodigiously long tail!
and a tongue like that of a man.
These birds are extremely learned
and not only are they able to speak,
they answer one another correctly.
Although most Europeans laugh at this
I myself have no doubt of it.

I do sometimes question what I hear,
but more often than not I can be persuaded.
How about you?

I think Prester John was the Christian ruler of Abyssinia
despite those who say the priest-kings in Saint Thomas'
meditation were his prototype. He was related, I believe,
to Yeliu Tashi, a chief of the Turki people called Kara Khitai
who lived in the north of Tien-shan during the 12th century.
Some of these people were Buddhists, true, but others

were known to be Christians; and there are many stories
of an immense Nestorian empire which flourished in Asia
during this dark epoch. I don't blame you for being skeptical
but listen: in the 17th century several Catholic missionaries
went to China, one of whom was a certain Father Trigault
who settled in the city of Singanfu, capital of the province
of Shen-si. While Father Trigault's house was being built
the laborers happened to dig up an ancient stone tablet
surmounted by a Nestorian cross embellished with flowers
and covered with Chinese calligraphy from the 8th century
which testified to the spread of the illustrious *Tach-in*
religion throughout the Middle Kingdom. Now what do you
say? Just in case you don't know, *Tach-in* is a word signifying
Christianity.

One must be careful about interpreting the past
but occasionally we feel confident. For instance:
when Prester John goes to war a cross made of wood
is carried in front of him, together with a gold basin
full of ordinary dirt in recognition of the fact that
his domain is earthly and his corpse will molder.

Pope Alexander III in 1177 composed a letter
to Prester John, whom he addressed as *Magnificus
Rex Indorum, Sacerdotum sanctissimus*, entrusting it
to his personal physician, Magister Philippus,
although neither of them nor anybody else
knew where or how it should be delivered.
Nonetheless, Magister Philippus boldly set out
and at this juncture disappears from history.
As a result, I'm led to agree with Quevedo
who holds the world to be a nightmare, all's chaos
and Fortune delights in making fools of men.

I also agree with an observation of Paracelsus
that prophets are ridiculed for their simplicity;
at the same time, they do stand closer to God.

Philippus Theophrastus Aureolus Bombastus ab Hohenheim,
called Paracelsus, was quite as curious as he was talented.

Late in life for some obscure reason he began to fast,
gave away his clothes and money, renounced his studies
and abstained from the crucible. His last days
he spent with the poor, meditating, preaching
and writing. It is claimed he wrote furiously
—not as I do, methodically, but obsessed by a need
to revise his ideas and assimilate fresh problems.
Now, four centuries after Paracelsus' death
I am translating the final chapters of his life.
I must admit I find them defective, disparate and
contradictory, lacking clarity or depth. The style,
for what it's worth, betrays a disturbed conscience
harried and reckless in its search for salvation.
For these reasons, together with a few others
not fit to discuss, I doubt if he is my equal.
Still, he it was who enunciated the brief principle
which guides me: *No man becomes a master at home
nor finds his teacher behind the stove.*

Certain men contribute factual bits of knowledge
to the whole and other invent techniques
facilitating our mastery of the universe;
but there are others that struggle with truth
too early, before understanding has ripened
or burst into the fruits of formulation.
Such men always lust after the fullest truth
when it would be much easier to compromise;
they would rather be mistaken in their search
than be correct without anguish. Good, I say.
Qui vit sans folie n'est pas si sage qu'il croit.

We may risk salvation as unquestionably as Faustus,
knight-errant of science who traveled everywhere
and studied all books—all without satisfaction
until at last he agreed to the Devil's demand,
which gave him power over space and matter
so that he was able to draw wine out of dry wood,
ride a barrel up the steps of Auerbach's cellar
and create the homunculus. But at Faustus' side
no matter where he went a black poodle trotted,

waiting to run off with his soul. Freedom's price
is happiness, according to this malignant parable.

In Würzburg lived the famous alchemist and magus
Johannes Heidenberg of Tritheim, called Trithemius,
Abbot of Sponheim, who understood the cabala
and a majority of occult sciences, who taught ethics
as well as history, was a connoisseur of pottery,
developed a method to teach foreign languages
in a few short lessons, conversed with friends
who were absent, conceived stupefying devices
that would make most modern inventions superfluous,
and called back the ghost of Mary of Burgundy
for the benefit of her husband, Maximilian.
Furthermore, he denied the existence of witches
and rigorously defended victims of the Inquisition.
His superiors, mordantly suspicious of cryptogrammata,
ciphers and unique prescriptions, accused him
of nefarious magic and removed him from the abbey.
However singular this abbot's method might have been
his recompense sounds all too familiar.

The orthodox John Donne accused Theophrastus
of following infernal orders with mineral and fire.
Magic flourishes in every climate. Now, if you will,
think of something contemporary.

Perfume, whistling,
bursts of music, burnt feathers,
apparitions . . .

I've never doubted that vermin originate
from the putrefaction of organic matter
or that a magnet when rubbed with leek
loses strength. I take it for granted
that to create a tree I condemn a seed to rot.
I say that the soul of a man, the marrow
of his backbone, congeals when he dies
and is metamorphosed into a serpent,
which explains why snakes are found near tombs.

I know that the air about us is thick with demons
—thicker than bottle-flies in August.
Does not sweet milk sour when a hag passes?
Do not dreams predict the deaths of relatives?

I advise you to look upon all things
prudently, and with circumspection;
earth's the home of difficulties.

I suggest that you avoid the presence of Deeves,
which wander across the desert uttering horrible cries.
By their horns and tails, resembling those of animals,
you will certainly recognize them. As I say,
be careful to avoid them; but if you cannot, remember
that being part human they are amenable to magic.

I recommend a strong drink called Coffee
that I tasted in the land of the Turks.
It's named for a berry, quite black
and bitter as soot, which they serve
as hot as they can suffer. Many hours
these Turks spend in their Coffee-houses
drinking and talking and so on and so on,
because this beverage procures alacrity
and assists digestion.

Here's a little advice concerning Sleep
which is known to moisten and fatten the body,
as you can see from dormice and Alpine mice
that sleep through the winter as soft as butter.
Usually it's best three hours after supper
when meat is settling toward the stomach,
and it's best to sleep on your right side
so that the liver remains underneath
to heat the stomach like a fire under a kettle.
It's all right to go to sleep on your belly
but never on your back. Seven or eight hours
should be enough. To lie overlong in bed
without sleep for the sake of inventing dreams
is wicked and pernicious.

Why do you smile? *Quid rides?*
Mutato nomine, de te fabula narratur.

Let me warn you: Don't lapse into the vulgar practice
of decrying what you don't comprehend. Look,
is it not by submission of the mind to diverse
possibilities that you earn the privilege of choice?
And without choice, my friend, what are you?

I realize that I say things which an uncharitable reader
might find fault with as personal, but you should understand
that we're not attending to formal business or listening
to a symphony with contrasting movements, nor to an operatic
work with an overture, arias, recitatives and a finale.
If I were to express our little discussion in musical terms
I would perhaps suggest that it modulates from theme
to theme, changing tempo and key, falling into reverie
yet always preserving its onward feeling compounded
of oneiric elements.

By the way, have I told you my name?
Have I shown you my credentials?
Do you suspect me of being an imposter?
I'll disclose everything, all in good time.
For now let's just say I'm a plowman
of—oh, let's say Bohemia, dispensing
wisdom as I work and travel. Say my plow
is the sharpened feather of a bird.
You don't need to know anything else.

Bright perceptions flicker. Old enmities,
new and enlightening affinit . . .

No, wait. Listen. I've thought it over
and I've decided to tell you the truth.
I've challenged Death to a game of chess
because He abducted Elizabeth, my wife,
and I am Death's indestructible opponent.
By a variety of devices I outwit Him,
but once in a while his suggestive fingers

brush my lips. I swallow and cough
and feel obligated to move:

N-Q2.
P-QB4.

Morning. January light down a leaded window.
I seat myself cross-legged on the mosaic floor
to reflect as women do, with images. Where I was
or what happened during the night I've no idea.
My friends laugh and say I shivered like a wet dog;
they insist that I barked and howled, whined,
leapt suddenly over a chair snapping at nothing.
They tell me I tried to swim in a puddle of urine.
I don't remember. I've swept away the experience;
it's useless to sift the past.

Listen. I propose that every library and archive
be burned, permitting life to seek a new direction.
In other words, I'm not roped to a stake like a pig;
traditions mean less than prehistoric arrowheads.
After all, my friend, the world's differently defined
in differing lands.

Who's to say that the tribesmen of Alor are incorrect
if they bury a person we would consider alive?

The people of Teber eat their parents' corpses
so the carcasses won't be attacked by worms;
and out of the skulls they fashion drinking cups,
recalling life's joys to their precious dead.
Maybe they know more than we do.

The people of America equate death with salvation,
but who could prove they were misdirected?

As you can see, my disposition's liberal; however
I do sometimes grow suspicious, even conservative.

I've heard that a Negro's brain is, on the average,
a bit smaller than the brain of a Caucasian. Perhaps.
And the latter's brain is, usually, a trifle smaller
than that of an Eskimo, a Kaffir or one of the Amaxosa.
I think it's possible. But as for the Sioux being Aryan,
let's try a little *vierhändig*.

Such baroque music leads to Comte Joseph de Gobineau
whose thesis of anthropological superiority in four
humorless volumes: *The Inequality of Human Races*
fascinated Richard Wagner, whose son-in-law
Houston Chamberlain published a subsequent installment.
What happened next was inevitable. *Weltmacht oder . . .*

Maidanek: 1,380,000.

Nietzsche, it would seem, has been rather maligned.
Consider that he opposed nationalism, anti-Semitism,
standing armies and the German Republic. Martin Luther
on the contrary suggested stabling Jews like gypsies,
burning their schools, synagogues, etc. Incidentally
note with what ease a priest's gesture of benediction
may be inverted—becoming the sign of malediction.
But as for Luther, shouldn't such a man be indicted?

Eloïm! Essaïm! Frigativi et appellavi!

Listen! Listen! The International Tribunal
has reassembled at Nuremberg:

1. *The policy of the American Government as implemented
by the Central Intelligence Agency was the calculated
and systematic execution of noncombatants in Quang Ngai
province under the code name "Operation Phoenix."*

2. *The thumbs of prisoners were tied together behind their
back, the mouth and eyes sealed with adhesive tape, a halter
looped about the neck, and each numbered with a white plastic
ticket. Some choked to death on their own vomit.*

3. *The bodies of sixteen women and children who were killed*
by United States Marines of the First Battalion, Seventh
Regiment, First Division, were dismembered with knives.

4. *he United States antipersonnel mine was designed to*
maim rather than to kill, because a corpse requires no
attention whereas rescue attempts may be directed toward
still-living casualties, thus providing secondary targets. It
was designed to hop approximately three feet into the air
before exploding with the deliberate purpose of destroying
the genitals. The charge consists of triangularly-shaped strips
of metal because American technicians learned that triangular
wounds not only are ugly and demoralizing, but are the most
difficult to heal.

Oh, my notebook's full of things. Nor do I forget much.
I remember when the American Legion exchanged greetings
with Mussolini, and a resolution expressing gratitude
to Il Duce for his efforts on behalf of Legion activities
in Italy was presented to the Fascist ambassador.

I remember Churchill addressing the House of Commons
with these words: "If I had to choose between Communism
and Nazism, I would choose Nazism."

Let's go back a bit. The cargo of the *Lusitania*
included 11 tons of black powder, 173 tons
of rifle ammunition and 2,400 cases of cartridges
for the British. Now this isn't exactly news,
but some people think it makes a difference.

Postwar investigations disclosed no authenticated
instance of Boches amputating the hands of Belgian
children, although it made a marvelous poster.

Do you think Germans boil corpses for use as fertilizer?
Brigadier General Charteris, Chief of British Intelligence,
said during a speech to the National Arts Club of New York
that he, himself, invented the charge. Since then, of course,
the Germans have had some use for vats.

Listen. Do you think the evils that afflict us
are conceived within, nourished by our own vitals?

Well, chances are you follow me like those patient Jews
sifting burnt leaves for the footprints of fugitive Nazis.
Those tenacious survivors and I agree it's not just foolish
but dangerous to skip the past.

Look, suppose we get down to business. I'm after
Colonel Giteau. I'll catch up with him sometime,
someplace—in the Sonora desert or in the hallway
of a Zurich apartment. He might even ring my bell
one morning while I'm reading the paper. He can't escape
and he and I both know it. Who escapes his destiny?

People will tell you that whatever happens to a man
was fixed at birth by the sutures of his skull,
but this isn't so. We always have a choice.
We walk from Hell to Paradise across a bridge
—a bridge narrower than the blade of a Damascus sword
or finer than the hair of an angel. *Domine, dirige . . .*

Miracles of the Soul, my friend, are greater
than those of Heaven.

Listen, here's a strange story. After the Apostle Philip
had converted Gaul a devoted company of his followers
led by Joseph of Arimathea was sent to colonize Britain.
Now, on a rise not far from Glastonbury close by the Tor
Joseph stopped to pray, and his staff took root and budded.
Because of this miracle King Arviragus gave Joseph the land,
and here he built the first Christian church in Britain.
His rooted staff, as you probably know, is the Glastonbury
Thorn which flowers each Christmas to honor Christ's birth.
You'll meet cynics who call this an ecclesiastic fable,
but they've got a lot to learn.

Don't misunderstand. I don't recommend naïve acceptance.
Be skeptical if skepticism's appropriate. For instance,
Biblical scholars examining the Hebrew text of Genesis
have discovered that the legend of Noah is a composite.

Originally there were two narratives, differing in detail,
which were artfully combined by anonymous Jewish scribes
about 500 B.C. Prudent men therefore read the Bible
critically.

Archaeologists in Mesopotamia uncovered a Sumerian
narrative on baked clay tablets telling about a man
who was warned by a god that a vast flood was imminent.
The god advised him to construct a boat and to take aboard
not only his wife and children, but his domestic animals.
Later it rained and rained until the earth was hidden
by water, and when the boat eventually touched ground
the Sumerian released a raven, a swallow and a dove.
Still later, he himself emerged and built an altar
where he offered a sacrifice.

Against the mound of Ur lies a deposit of silt
11 feet thick, which means that the water at this point
was 25 feet deep, or 15 cubits—the Flood's depth
according to Genesis. Mesopotamia, of course, is flat
and a flood of such magnitude at the village of Ur
would have inundated 30,000 square miles.
That is, as far as anybody could see.

Lyonesse, too, was overwhelmed by water—its one survivor
Trevilian, who leapt on a horse and fled to the mainland.
Proof of this legend endures on the Trevilian coat-of-arms
which shows a horse issuing from the sea.

At one time all of Great Britain was under water.
Thick beds of clay, gravel and sand were deposited
on the submerged island. Geologists refer to this
as the Northern Drift, and when the land did emerge
it wore these water deposits like a heavy garment.
Some people suspect that Germany, too, will one day
lift herself from beneath the surface. God help us.
I'd rather not think about it.

Reality is anathema. I spend my days reading
fabulous stories. I'm engrossed by Tacitus
who speaks of islands beyond the Guiones,

and of a motionless body of water beyond them
which bounds and encloses our terrestrial disk.
The presence of this ocean may be verified,
he claims, by the setting sun whose last gleam
endures until morning with dazzling radiance.
So far reaches the world we know, but no farther.

According to Plato, Atlantis lies outside the port of Gades;
but my neighbor, who is a marine biologist, disagrees.
He and some other scientists sounded the ocean bed nearby
and measured a layer of pelagic red clay which consisted
principally of the shells of plankton. It was 11,000' thick.
What this means is that approximately 500 million years
must have elapsed since the bed of the Atlantic off Gades
was last exposed, because this sediment is being deposited
at the rate of 3/10" every 1,000 years. Atlantis' location,
therefore, it pretty much anybody's guess.

The Canary Islands represent the Hesperides
in the opinion of most scholars, while the giant Atlas
is embodied by the peak of Teneriffe. Hercules'
golden apples, they've decided, are easy to find:
pick the golden yellow fruit of *Arbutus canariensis*,
our familiar strawberry tree.

Anthropologists have traced the Golden Fleece
to sheep hides staked in a stream by natives of Phasis
who periodically comb the hides for gold particles
adhering to the wool. *Mirabile dictu!*

Pliny, speaking of the outermost land called Thule,
would have us believe that during the solstice
when the sun passes through the sign of the Crab
there's no night. He also claims that during winter
a single night lasts six months. Well, my friend,
we don't yet know what Pliny's remarks symbolize
but if you take them literally you're gullible.

Don't misinterpret me. I do admit the existence
of natural marvels. We read in the 13th century

Landnámabók, for example, that when Northmen
first arrived in Iceland they found the country
thick with trees! And Christians were living there
whom the Vikings called *papar*, who departed
rather than live with a community of heathen,
and left behind a number of crosiers and bells
and Irish books. But as to where these people went
the *Landnámabók* is silent.

Ancient manuscripts in the abbeys of Strata Florida
and Conway mention the great Welsh King Madoc
sailing around the south of Ireland in 1170.
"He came to a beautiful country west of the sea"
by these accounts, were he left many of his people.
Madoc later reembarked with hundreds of colonists
in ten ships, so he must have been deeply excited.
But that's all we know; history says nothing more.

Rumors of a people with fair skin
living in the wilderness of America
reached the *courreurs du bois* so frequently
that Jean Nicolet, expecting to meet them,
packed a silk robe in his birchbark canoe;
he thought these people must be Chinese
who could show him the mysterious passage
leading out of one world into another.
Many of us dream Jean Nicolet's dream.

In 1540 the crew of a German merchant ship
blown by strong winds into a Greenland fjord
saw a dead European lying on an island
with his face to the frozen earth. His clothing
of sealskin and frieze had a well-sewn hood
and beside him lay a dagger, bent and thin
from constant sharpening. This was the corpse
of the last Viking colonist in the New World
whom there had been nobody left alive to bury.
Yet once again our story seems incomplete;
we don't know what kind of service he was given
or if the Germans just left him there.

After World War I an archaeological commission
was dispatched to Greenland by the Danish government
to look for the ruins of two medieval settlements
which were known as Vestribyggd and Eystribyggd.
Church foundations, together with evidence of
several farms—the fields and gardens smothered
by weeds and horsehair oats—were discovered
on the western littoral. There, too, lay the Vikings:
Bishop Jon Smyrill, called the Sparrowhawk,
wearing his ring and holding a crosier
carved from the tusk of a walrus by his wife
Margret; the girl Ingibjourg, dead eight centuries,
her grave enclosed by a carved sandstone fence;
Ozuur Asbjarnarson, who had died on some island
during winter and was buried in unhallowed ground
with a stake standing vertically above his chest
so that when spring came and the ice melted
it could be with drawn and consecrated water
poured into the hole by a priest. Also revealed
was the history of a woman called Gudveig
who died at sea and was buried like a sailor,
sewn into sackcloth with a stone at her feet;
her grave was empty except for a rune rod
which served as a proxy, because the sea
isn't hallowed—it's the abode of the Devil.
And there were children's graves, quite a few.
Each of the children was holding a cross
and beside their bodies lay simple toys.
All of this turned up at the sites of Vestribyggd,
which means the western settlement, and Eystribyggd,
which refers to the eastern. So, having uncovered
what they were looking for, the archaeologists
collected a number of the most informative artifacts
and sailed home.

One other thing about these medieval Vikings:
they were small and grotesquely crippled.
They had suffered from malnutrition, rickets
and tuberculosis and few had lived past twenty.
Just the same, they were dressed to the teeth

in accordance with European notions of that period
—although in a thick coarse woolen frieze
manufactured by the colonists themselves
rather than in dyed silk or Italian velvet.
They had fashioned this rough cloth into caps
and the surcoats of the late Middle Ages,
into knee-length cothards and hoods with a queue
which we recognize from the descriptions of Dante
or Petrarch, into the tall Burgundian headgear
pictured by Memling and other Flemish artists.
Until the very end these wretched starving dwarfs
had done their best to keep in style.

A few minutes ago my brother came into the room
to ask what I was doing. I said that in 1630 A.D.
the main archives of the church at Skalholt
were destroyed by fire, and we are indebted
to Bishop Oddson who re-created many documents
from memory. I'm just doing the same, I added,
otherwise we'd lose a great deal of information.
He stared at me with a look of insane mistrust
but he went away, thank God. I say thank God
because I'm anxious to continue. Neither of us,
I suspect, boasts a surplus of time.

P-KN3.
N-QB3.

Now pay attention. A race of blue-eyed Nordic
savages called Guanches, whose origin
has never been established, was discovered
several centuries ago living on two islands
not far above the equator. It's conjectured
that they were the descendants of Goths
or Vandals cast out of the sea by accident.
In any event, they've disappeared. What little
we learn not only arrives too late but seems
pathetically insufficient, while so many things
altogether elude us—beating brilliantly forward
like the wings of migratory butterflies.

The Norse King Roger of Sicily and a learned Arab
philosopher, physician and geographer named Ibn Idrisi
collaborated on three works summarizing the knowledge
of their age: a celestial sphere, a silver disk
representing the world and a geographical treatise
titled *Al Rojari*. Although Greenland and Vinland
were familiar by tradition, neither was delineated
on the map or was mentioned in the treatise
because so little of what they had been told
could be authenticated. Ireland and the Canaries,
therefore, became the western limit of the world.
They were cognizant of Japan to the east,
but ignored Polynesia even though these islands
had been described during the 10th century
by Ali Masudi in his celebrated *Murudsh al-Dhabab*
or *Meadow of Gold*. Ibn Idrisi and King Roger
evidently thought Polynesia sounded implausible.
To the north they admitted Archangel, the lakes
Ladoga and Onega and the rivers Volga, Don,
Dniester and Dnieper. They knew about Lake Bakal,
the Himalayas and something of Tibet. To the south,
however, they were convinced of very little
below Morocco and decided to omit curious tales
of rivers, jungles, mountains and fanciful deserts.
In other words, here were two men as cautious
as they were intelligent who mistrusted shadows.
Men so blessed are unusual and always welcome.

A Greek from Marseille, Pytheas, an astronomer
of impeccable reputation during the 3rd century
before Christ, fitted out a ship with his own money
to go in search of knowledge. When he returned
he wrote a prolix account of his discoveries.
Although his manuscript seems to have been lost
we have the word of a certain Polybius who read it
and has this to say about the inquisitive astronomer:
Pytheas sailed north from the Pillars of Hercules
to the Tin Islands where he disembarked
and spent some time wandering about on foot
observing the people and comparing them with Greeks.

He found that they drank mead instead of wine
and lived in caves or lake villages. They wore
horned helmets and enameled bronze bracelets
and carried shields. They knew about wheeled carts,
how to domesticate animals, the smelting of ore,
and where to look for amber along the beaches
of Helgoland. After leaving these Tin Islands,
Polybius tells us, Pytheas sailed six days north
to Thule—wherever that was. Iceland? Norway?
In any case, here he saw something so astounding
that when he got home it made his reputation
as a liar. After all, a sea that's frozen?

What isn't thought incredible at first?
Quid non miraculo est
cum primum in notitiam venit?

Captain Warren, master of the Greenland whaler *Herald*,
reported a startling apparition that bore down on him
out of the mist-shrouded north as the *Herald* lay becalmed:
a vessel sheathed in ice—its spars, sails and ropes
glittering malignantly, and not a sound could be heard
except the creak of timber. Captain Warren, accompanied
by several of his crew, discovered after going aboard
that she was the *Octavius* out of England, eastbound
on the China trade. Twenty-eight dead men wrapped in
blankets were found in the forecastle, each man on his bunk
as though asleep, and in the master's cabin the Captain
slouched in his chair, a quill pen on the table
next to his right hand and the logbook lying open.
Every entry was legible, but not one word to explain
her position—why she had sailed into the Arctic.
Captain Warren, a practical man, professed himself
mystified. My guess is that the *Octavius'* master,
exhausted by the monotonous economics of his life,
had been seeking the Northwest Passage.

The *Marlborough* out of Glasgow, homeward bound
from New Zealand with a cargo of meat and wool,
was reported lost near the Straits of Magellan;

but seamen in southern latitudes still sight her
—her sails shaggy with moss, her decks rotting,
six skeletons sprawled on the bridge and another
at the helm. If she ever reaches Glasgow, they say,
a plague will settle on Scotland. Maybe it's true.
The sea and the earth hold plenty of secrets.

We know that Columbus wrote a full account of his voyage
on a parchment scroll which he wrapped in waterproof cloth
and placed in an ironbound barrel on February 14th, 1493.
So, by your leave, take a moment to imagine
what might come riding down the high Atlantic waves
if this barrel washed ashore.

Lat. 16.14 N.; Long. 49.03 W.
The compass drifts, stories change;
relationships arrange themselves
only in order to rearrange themselves
through some logic of their own.

I used to collect sailing schedules and maps
and contemplate traveling suits and valises,
and talk about the various foreign countries
I meant to visit; but actually leaving
turned out to be unexpectedly difficult.
Consequently I watched winter come and go,
spring, summer and autumn. Nothing's easier,
believe me.

Today is my 36th birthday and tomorrow
when my wife wakes up I won't be here.
As for my destination—Poland, Luxembourg,
the Dalmatian coast—who knows? Possibly
some island spun with turquoise currents
where night carries the odor of nutmeg.
This isn't her fault, you understand;
different men need different pleasures.

It occurs to me as I watch my wife sleeping
that no reflections disturb the antique beauty
of her face. Why should I feel dissatisfied?

She's like those marble figures we meet
suddenly in the alcoves of provincial museums
titled *Proserpina* or *Ceres*, half-concealed
because their plump grace seems affected
and their polished features too perfect.

People complain that I'm not just unkind, but unfair
to women. I don't think so; in fact, quite the opposite.
They're made of glass, my friend. *Es de vidrio la mujer.*

Women are known to become excited at funerals, executions
and scenes of martyrdom; history's leaves are stained
with instances of their erratic, licentious behavior
while men escorting them behaved with propriety
and commendable rectitude.

Women are often attacked by nervousness. The nuns of Acre,
for example, mutilated themselves as soon as the fortress
was captured by Saracens. Those in the Coldingham convent,
told of Danish soldiers approaching, sliced off each others'
lips and noses.

The flux and reflux of their imagination urges women
to behave in curious ways. Magdalen, wife of Louis XI,
coming across the King's chaplain asleep, embraced him
fervently and kissed him, explaining to her companions
that she embraced not an ugly old man, which in fact
he was, but the lustrous unfaded beauty of his soul.

And why should it be that among the greatest mystics
only the women, Saint Ignatius Loyola excepted,
have been visionaries? Think about Catherine of Siena,
Marie of the Incarnation, Mechtilde of Hackeborn,
Elizabeth of Schönau, Julian of Norwich and others.
For the most part, like oceans or tidal pools,
women keep their vital secrets.

How women are able to assess a man's possibilities
with one glance is not understood, but that they do so
is commonly admitted. They can interpret hands,
eyes, gait and many other things. Above all else

they are sensitive to the meanings of a deep voice.
However, such information won't do you any good
when dealing with women because of a powerful
comprehension between the sexes. In other words,
flesh acknowledges flesh, denying or consenting.

Perhaps the only thing I can tell you
which might prove to be of some faint value
is that he who asks timidly has made denial easy.
Qui timide rogat, docet negare.

If these deviations disconcert you,
too bad. Just as shifts of mood
or tempo are essential to a symphony,
so I scatter notes as I please. But observe
how invariably I select the transparent wash
of Debussy to the garish pigment of
—oh, say *Scheherazade*. Why? Because
barbaric rhythms distress and burn my delicate ear.

My neighbor the musician says I remind him of Bartók
who had a reputation for being inexpressive and aloof.
Then, too, it seems that Bartók had a skin disease
which covered him with sores, making him uncomfortable
in the presence of everyone except his mother. All right,
I admit to similarities; no doubt my grotesque appearance
must be as unmistakable as my temperament. But remember:
great men are permitted grievous faults.

Because of my intellect my stepfather hates me.
I despise him because of the way he eats his soup.
At times I mention my genius, which breaks apart
old forms to create the new. He responds without much wit
that while I may be precocious I'm as weak as a flower.
He attempts to parody me by mumbling and sneering,
accuses me of sloth, and proposes that one fine day
everybody will recognize and salute the power I have
of foreseeing my own wretchedness. Yet as he addresses me
he turns half-aside.

I've just now been asked to name a person I admire.
The question's difficult and deserves some thought.
If an immediate answer were required I suppose I'd say
I admire nobody, although I've met one or two I respect.
Here's the thing: admiration connotes subservience,
respect implies an equal and complementary distance.

I respect the King of Thrace who broke and exquisite present
deliberately, so it couldn't be broken by accident.

I respect the French theoretical astronomer
Urbain J. J. Leverrier, for his *sang-froid*.
Here's what happened. After the discovery of Uranus
by Herschel, and the plotting of the planet's orbit,
a slight irregularity in its course was noted;
and Leverrier, who spent almost a year calculating,
concluded that the gravitational attraction of
some unknown body should account for the eccentricity.
He therefore wrote to a German, one Johann Galle,
asking him to study a particular area of the sky.
Now, this letter was delivered to Galle in Berlin
during his own birthday party, but he went at once
to his laboratory where in just a few minutes
he was able to locate the previously undetected object.
Leverrier, informed that the body he predicated
did in fact exist, was rather pleased. However,
since he now knew beyond doubt that it was there
he never bothered to have a look at it. *Chapeaux bas!*

As to those I abhor—well, the Potomac's a dirty river
and fat geese fly a clumsy skein. The reference is obvious,
or perhaps it isn't. In the extravagance of my conceit
am I addressing a barbarian?

Translate the following:
Kennst du das Land wo die Zitr . . .

Oh, never mind. As you've probably guessed
I used to be in the Army. They put me to work
answering letters of inquiry. Well, at first

I was troubled and tried to sound sympathetic,
but sooner or later every job becomes a bore
so I'd just scribble "Deceased" on the envelopes
and mail them back. In fact, I got so I could write
while listening to music or with a cigarette
in my teeth and one eye shut against the smoke.
Kings make mistakes, they say, and the Greeks
get punished.

United States aircrewmen wear this message
on their flight jackets. Listen:
I am an American and do not speak your language.
I need food, shelter, assistance.
I will not harm you.
I bear no malice toward your people.
If you will help me you will be rewarded.
What do you think, how much is true?
How much is false?

Listen. I heard just a little while ago
that U.S. fighter bombers attacked
and destroyed a primary school,
killing eight children.

Is the dream dead?
Is Nixon mad?

Does lust of dominion light a candle
in the heart? Do dragons assault elephants
to drink their blood? Is it the other way around?
Is the combustion of a corpse a streaming-forth of phlogiston?
Some few things I consider to be explicable;
others exceed our comprehension.

Can the soul of one just dead enter a living soul
to sustain and instruct? Frankly, I don't know.
I admit I'm bewildered and frightened.

The true ground of medicine is love, I think;
and that which is finite is evil, for one drop

of vinegar can certainly sour a barrel of wine.
If you believe everything you hear, of course,
you're a fool. What's important is to discriminate.

Listen. Diseases of the mind and of the body
wander the total length of the world
and whoever wishes fully to understand them
has little time for a nap next to the stove.
As I say, you must separate fact from fraud;
if you decide to dispute this, my friend,
goodby.

William Gilbert, in his posthumous treatise
titled *A New Philosophy of our Sublunary World*,
states that the existence of elements is a fable:
the action of the sun on the earth generates all.
Minerals grow from the juices of that great seminary
Earth; Nature makes bodies, not elements or mixtures,
and each of us is guided by subtle attractions.
There's some truth here, but be cautious.
Not all of Nature's hints require elaboration.
She has created orchids in the shape of testicles
so that their juices may restitute our lewdness;
she has made both liverwort and kidneywort
with leaves in the shape of the parts they cure;
she indicates the age of a stag by his antlers.

As to the stars, you may be told they determine
nothing, neither do they suggest much,
and we are no more bound by their influence
than are they by ours; yet the epidemic
of syphilis that in 1494 ravaged Europe
was caused by a conjunction of three planets.

Is not the phoenix born of a horse's carcass?
Can't water be found with the aid of divining rods?
Haven't we built a great wall against our enemies?

Perhaps you consider my questions absurd. If so,
why? Remember Archytas, who constructed a dove

that flew in circles by the use of compressed air
five centuries before Christ. In other words,
Credo quia absurdum est.

Friend, name what you like, nothing I've named
is half as absurd as today. Listen: the beaver,
when he is hunted, bites off his own testicles
because he assumes that's why his body is wanted;
America sweeps the palace of King Savang Vatthana
to dissuade him from negotiating with Communists.

The Derbikkai who inhabit the Caspian littoral
punish every crime with death, according to Strabo;
Egyptian pilots following American instructions
drop canisters of poison gas on Yetaf.

I could continue, but to what purpose?
The Church takes no action against a priest
who goes mad, nor do we. Vain plays, useless words
—a squabble of cap and bells. Possibly Calvin's
49th sermon on Deuteronomy would be appropriate:
We seek that God should serve our mad appetites
and that He should be as though subject to ourselves.

Have we grown as near to barbarism
as steel is to rust?

Do we resemble some acephalous beast?

Historians tell us that 21 civilizations
lie in history's grave. Of this number
2 fell beneath foreign attacks, 19 decayed.
Ora pr . . .

I've seen the shadow of an hourglass
and heard the whisper of a scythe.
What should I do when my turn comes?
If you know, we two might travel
up and down the dusty ways, across
earth's latitude and longitude forever.
Be quick, if you're my friend tell me:

B-N2.
N-B3.

All at once it's evening. I've just finished supper
and begun my usual cigar. In the April darkness
a warm rain drips noiselessly from the awning.
The gleaming wet tiles of the nearby Vavin métro
suggest an exit from some immaculate mausoleum.
A young fire-eater struts beside the steps,
naked to the waist—his sleek feminine torso
green with tattoos. Dramatically he waves a torch,
out of his stretched mouth an orange flame curls
like a dragon's tongue. Such vivid dreams we hold.
Dame des cieulx, regente terrienne, emperiere des
infernaux palus, recevez moy, vostre humble chrest...

An oil portrait of me hangs in a corridor of the Louvre,
painted some years ago. It shows a man of unmistakable
substance, broad and strong, with purplish Negroid lips,
a cleft chin, a noble brow, dark impatient luminous eyes
and glossy ringlets coiling artfully about his shoulders.
At the time I sat for the artist I had only just returned
from South America and I was anticipating other honors
to cap my career. Since those days, however, the king
who subsidized my explorations has been deposed
by Republicans who see little but immediate civil needs.
They are, I think, purblind governors hostile to whatever
promises no quick payment. And as for my fellow citizens,
men bolder than myself might explore the moon
yet come home to popular ridicule.

If the stature of a man may be measured by his travels
I would be hard to overlook. Between Paris and Fiji
there must not be twelve countries I've yet to visit.
I walked across primitive lands festooned with beliefs
so incredible that if I attempted to summarize them
civilized people would laugh and call me a charlatan.
In the province of Mobar I have seen a gilded idol
with a ribbon about its neck to which the Indians go
on pilgrimage, just as Christians do unto Saint Peter.
Some journey with halters, others with bound hands,

others with knives sticking in their arms and legs,
and if the tormented flesh festers they esteem it holy
because they think their god is well pleased. Also
I have watched men throw themselves under the wheels
of a chariot that bears the god from its golden temple,
avowing that they die for a noble cause.

I have been to see the Coords, descended from Parthians,
who live not far from Aleppo and worship the Devil
because they say God is good and does not hurt anybody,
but the Devil is wicked and so we should please him.

I have studied the religion of the Aztecs,
which possesses so many Christian features
that Spanish priests decry it as a bogus imitation,
conceived and presented to them by the Devil
in order to destroy their souls. True or not,
certain secular accomplishments of these savages
excite such wonder that we are almost envious.

In Quiriguá, which is near Copán, stands a pillar
covered with lengthy bands of hieroglyphics
reckoning a date ninety million years ago,
carved by a now degenerate race called Maya.
Only by means of the abstract cipher zero,
realized by these people before it was understood
in Asia, could such a mathematical problem
be solved and, assisted by the movable cipher
which is the symbol of absence, be recorded.

In Peru is an aqueduct of hewn stone and cement
extending countless miles across sierras and rivers.
There also is an artificial garden whose soil
is composed of the very finest flakes of gold,
with maize stalks simulated in gold, even the stems
and cobs and leaves—all gold. And a flock of sheep
or *llamas*, as large as life, together with lambs
and shepherds. Everything everywhere is gold.
But sometimes you find piles of rock along the roads
built by the savages as memorials to their burden,

which demonstrates that they are capable of feeling,
contrary to what most people believe.

In its fullest glory the Egyptian Middle Kingdom
bloomed from Alexandria to the rapids of Assuan
at the delta, which is perhaps six hundred miles;
but the distance from the Purumauca fortress
on the north bank of the Maule river in Chile
into the Ancasmayo, marking the uppermost limit
of the great Inca domain, is five times as far.
And speaking of riches, my friend, the *quipus* say
seven million ounces of gold pour into Cuzco
annually. Not that I am obsessed by wealth,
you understand.

What attracts me more than money is primitive sculpture
such as I have excavated from the ruins of Huaca Prieta
—miniature gourds embellished with human visages
carved two thousand years before the birth of Christ,
or those elaborate ceramic figures from Teotihuacán
which repeated past patterns of a majestic civilization
until headdresses at length overwhelmed the sterile images,
as if the representation of splendor could in fact replace
its essence; much as we have observed papal inanities
precede the declining orb of Rome.

Turquoise mosaics from prehistoric Mexico
—*ornamenti dei barbari*—were broken apart
and refashioned in Florentine workshops
to satisfy the taste of Medici ladies.
Itzá is no more and Palenque is no more
where things were done that will not be again.
Mayapan is no more, our banner and pride.
All has passed. Nothing remains but the grave
of him who dug the grave.

Beginning with the year 12-House, which is to say
in the year of our Lord 1517, omens of doom appeared
to the Aztecs: a comet flashed like an ear of corn;
the great temple of Huitzilopochtli burst into fire;

lightning struck another temple; a second comet was seen
at midday; the lake of Tenochtitlan boiled; a woman
was heard to weep night after night; and in his net
a fisherman caught a crane the color of ashes
which held a mirror in its mouth. And Moctezuma
when he gazed into this mirror saw Spanish cavaliers
riding against his people.

Speculating on the origin of the Aztecs, Bartolomé de las
Casas wondered if their ancestors might be the lost tribes
of Israel. *Cuéntaselo a tu abuela!*

The first Bishop of Yucatán, Diego de Landa,
hoping to reduce Mayan glyphs to an alphabet,
carefully pronounced each letter as it was heard
in Spain, and requested an educated Maya
to draw a corresponding glyph. The results,
however, made little sense. For example,
after hearing de Landa speak the letter *b*
the Indian drew a picture of a foot,
because in his language the sound implied
either a journey or a narrow path.

Writing for the benefit of his sovereigns
in *Relación de las cosas de Yucatán*
Bishop de Landa remarks that the Indians
employ definite signs or letters
to record in their books their early history
and their lore. By means of such letters,
as well as by drawings and figures,
they understand their own story
and cause others to understand and to learn.
Quite a number of these books were found,
he adds, but because of their contents,
which consisted of nothing but superstition
and lies of the Devil, he burned them.

The *Codex Peresianus*, which dates from the decline
of the Classic Period and consists of prophecies
evidently based on the twenty-year *katun* cycle

and the twenty-times-twenty-year *baktun*,
was uncovered by one of my grandfather's friends
beneath a stack of wastepaper in the basement
of the Bibliothèque Nationale. On its wrapper
somebody had scribbled in 16th-century script: *Perez*.
That's all anybody has been able to learn.
Do kings suspect the destiny they leave behind?

Certain Spanish priests have identified Quetzalcoatl
as Saint Thomas Aquinas because of his whiteness
and beard, and because he wears the Maltese cross.
Others say this is not so, that he was the Messiah.
Still others claim that he was a shipwrecked Viking.
My own investigations lead me to think this benign god
was Noah; but it would take too long to tell you why.
Faith is essential.

I neither hope nor intend to embrace the whole,
merely to afford a hint of it—as Dêsiré Charnay
after having explored the ruins of Central America
concluded that the Toltecs were robust bearded men
with fair skin, yet refused to state specifically
where they were from. We are positive, nevertheless,
that strangely white Indians speaking fluent Welsh
once lived along the banks of the Mississippi
who may have been Prince Madoc's lost colonists,
and skeletons have been excavated in Kentucky
beneath brass-plated shields bearing the mermaid
and harp, emblematic of Wales.

Near the New York village of Lyons an old tree was felled
and axe marks were noticed very close to its center.
The age of this tree having been calculated at 460 years,
the marks must have been made during the 14th century
by a metal implement unknown to aborigines.

Juan de Torquemada who lived in the 17th century
mentions the ruins of a Chinese sailing vessel
weathering on a California beach. If it was Chinese
or not we have no way of determining at this date,

but it's a fact that when Columbus was in Galway
he saw corpses with Oriental features in an open boat
that had drifted halfway around the world.

I've studied the notes Columbus left on the margin
of Pliny's *Natural History*, which are in Spanish.
Only once did he attempt to write in Italian
although it's said he was Italian, and his mother's name
was Fontanarossa. Anyway, he was a Spaniard at heart
which is why I understand him. Italians puzzle me.
That's a digression, however. What I meant to say
was that my colleagues and I have established numerous
similarities between the customs of prehistoric Mexicans
and the early Chinese—none more startling than this:
both painted their funerary jades with red cinnabar.
The possibility of "coincidence" seems rather remote
in contrast to the inference, which is staggering.
Furthermore, we have agreed that a Buddhist priest
named Hoei-Shin, which means Universal Compassion,
reached the western coast of the American continent
sometime during the Tsi Dynasty, perhaps 499 A.D.
Conceivably you saw his portrait among the multitude
of terra cotta "smiling faces" excavated at Vera Cruz.

Now, the Chinese name for America is Fusang
because of a tree growing there in abundance
whose leaves are similar to the *Dryanda cordifolia*
and whose fruit resembles a pear, but is red,
and whose sprouts look like bamboo shoots.
But the name of this country is less important
than the remarkable nature of its punishments.
In Fusang or America, whichever you prefer,
a man judged guilty of any crime, no matter what,
is publicly showered with ashes and banished.
If he is a man of low rank he suffers by himself,
but the degradation extends to his children
if his rank happens to be high; and if exalted
his children are disgraced to the 7th generation.
As you can see, punishing evil with greater evil
is not restricted to the Orient.

Everywhere on earth crimes and punishments
reveal not only the nature of those who commit them
but of those who propose them. Later, perhaps,
I'll describe some of the horrors I've witnessed.
But first, because it's by travel or at least
by a knowledge of travel that reality regulates
the imagination and obligates us to look at things
as they actually exist instead of being distorted
by ignorance, you should hear about a voyage or two
or three.

A shaman of the Liu Sung Dynasty, Fa-Hsein,
walked from central China across the Gobi Desert
and the Hindu Kush through India to the Hooghly River
which enters the Bay of Bengal south of Calcutta.
Christians are forced to admit that by comparison
St. Paul's journeys melt away.

An Italian banking expert, Antonio Malfante,
investigated the Sahara as far as the Tuat oasis
on behalf of Centurione, a mercantile firm
quite influential at the time with branch offices
in Genoa, Caffa, Mallorca, Lisbon, Rouen, etc.
Anyway, writing to his friend Giovanni Marioni
the adventurous merchant reports that in Tuat
no one mistreats him, though he admits annoyance
because they often cry out with astonishment:
Behold! The Christian has a face like us!
In those days Mahometans thought all Christians
were deformed, a singularly persistent belief.

Kuyuk, the Mongol emperor, said to Benedict XII:
You consider yourselves to be Christians
and despise others. How do you know who deserves
God's mercy? Benedict's response, for better or worse,
has been lost.

Gregory X, hoping to convert Kublai Khan,
ordered William of Tripolis and Nicholas of Vicenza
to accompany Maffeo and Nicolo Polo.

But in Armenia at the Gulf of Alexandretta
both monks turned back, fearing for their lives.
God knows how history was affected.

An army of 20,000 German boys and girls
together with 30,000 French children
marched religiously toward the Mediterranean
in the 13th century after persuading themselves
that the water would divide in obedience
to their wishes and permit them to continue
unmolested as far as the gates of the Holy City.
All of them died or were sold into slavery
except for a few hundred German children
who eventually straggled back across the Alps.
Of the young French crusaders, one boy returned.
Mali principii malus finis.

In 1464 a half-mad Pope, Pius II,
set out on still another crusade,
traveling in a canopied litter,
and died at the port of embarkation
unaware that nobody had followed him.
Is this beginning to sound familiar?

Pope Leo IV was of the opinion that soldiers
who died in battle would be first to meet the joys
of Heaven. John VIII designated them holy martyrs,
provided they died while fighting for the Church
and were pure of heart.

Bohemond's warriors ate the flesh of Turks,
declaring it tastier than spiced peacock.
This, too, has contemporary reverberations.

Here's another: medieval Europeans regarded the Templars
not as gentle knights, but with almost as much fear
as they looked upon the Assassins. Can you guess why?

Let me explain. The U.S. antipersonnel "leaf bomb"
is a raggedly shaped little device customarily painted
in one of four colors, depending on the terrain:

deep red for clay, green for planted fields, off-white
for sandy soil and charcoal-colored for mud. So sensitive
are these miniature bombs that they can be triggered
by the touch of a child's foot.

Are you listening? There's a chemical laboratory
at Pine Bluff, Arkansas, where government technicians
devise bacteria and toxins suitable for infecting
millions of people anywhere in the world. A pamphlet
titled *Military Biology and Biological Agents*
lists a number of diseases which can be distributed
efficiently and quickly. Among them are cholera,
diphtheria, staphylococcus food poisoning, tetanus,
typhoid and gas gangrene.

Das Krieg ist lustig den unerfahrn…

The antique clock ticks. Wind lifts the curtain.
I remember a photograph of my uncle in uniform.
Now he sits and reads—usually about the Greeks
and Romans, how they quenched a need for violence
by watching animals in the hippodrome. He reads
uneasily, I think. I can't be sure. I turn each page
and wait for his signal. When I was in Hyderabad
I happened to see a leper with a blasted face
seated against a stone wall like a stitched bundle.
And my uncle sits destroyed in his favorite chair.

Men have false ideas, I think, about goodness
and justice, which explains why they worship false gods
individually or in concert.

Because men are by nature unequal
intellectually as well as morally,
few are capable of apprehending truth
despite assiduous preparation.
Let's put it like this: Lyndon Johnson
sent bombers to devastate North Vietnam
only after assurance from his generals
that not many civilians would be injured.

I've already told you I keep a journal of Abominations
in which I perpetuate the names of people I despise,
together with their acts or what they said. At times
instead of writing with ink I use either piss or blood.
A Congressman from Colorado named Peter Dominick
criticized the news media for directing attention
to U.S. soldiers murdering noncombatants at Song My.
Whether or not Dominick deserves to be included
I haven't decided, but you should know the sort he is.

Colonel Giteau, needless to say, has been immortalized;
I was his subordinate for quite a while.

I won't ignore the contribution of the Bundy brothers,
William and McGeorge. I have no intention of permitting
their names to fade like a medieval tapestry. Rusk, Rostow,
McNamara—I'll make sure nobody forgets what they did.

Thousands of names are in my journal right now
and the parade of candidates would astonish you.
I include those Pentagon officials responsible
for calling air strikes on Vietnamese villages
without warning in order to avoid "generating
additional refugees" as they euphemistically
express it. I include the amoral merchants,
of course. Dow Chemical, whose fiery products
are anathema to people halfway around the world,
might symbolize all of them. Incidentally, if a nation
is despised by its own citizens, what happens?

Look, the angle between branches around a tree trunk
remains constant in each type, and this angle
equals that between the principal vein of a leaf
and its subsidiary veins. Fractionally put, the numbers
follow a sequence which is known to mathematicians.
Perhaps you think this information is idle. It isn't.
Defoliation programs will become more effective.

A scientific assumption that the vertical thrust
of a hydrogen bomb would split the stratosphere
and allow the dissipation of radioactive krypton

proved correct. We were to be protected from this
lethal rain by the troposphere's natural umbrella.
Unfortunately, the design of the troposphere was
inadequately understood; it seems that a slight gap
exists between the polar and equatorial tropospheres
through which this radioactive material returned
to sweep the earth—falling on rivers, lakes, fields
and living creatures. So you see why we monitor
strontium in children's bones.

The missile known as *Poseidon*
is not only larger, but technically
advanced over its predecessor *Polaris*.
In diameter, payload, accur . . .

Josephus Grünpeck cries out:
When you perceive the miserable corruption
of the whole of Christendom, of all
praiseworthy customs, rules and laws,
the wretchedness of all classes,
the many pestilences, the changes
in this epoch, and the strange happenings,
you know that the end of the world is near.
And the waters of affliction will flow
over the whole of Christendom.
I have little reason to doubt it,
nor that Nuremberg awaits us.

N1-B3.
B-K2.

Death grows merry over His harvest!
Everything falls beneath Death's strokes
—the grass, the shoots, the ripening corn.
Thus we paint Sir Death in a joyful jig
on a wall of the Cemetery of the Innocents.

When the Huguenot town of Orange
fell to the Catholics its citizens
were hacked to pieces and roasted.
Naked women were hung in windows

as targets for devout musketeers,
leaves from their Geneva Bibles
pasted over the *mons veneris*.

Edward, when he had captured Berwick,
ordered eight thousand citizens butchered,
and burnt alive every Flemish trader.
This was on Good Friday, 1296.

Cromwell, on August 13th, 1649, at Drogheda
supervised the slaughter of two thousand people,
and those who had fled to a church for safety
were immolated when he set the building afire.

On the 13th of November, 1002,
which is called Saint Bryce's Day,
every Dane in England was murdered.

Genghis Khan slew 1,748,000 at Nishapûr.

Now let me tell you about Timur Beg
who, when he had captured Ispahan,
ordered its citizens to assemble.
Then he decapitated the men and the boys
and built a huge pyramid of their heads.
The women and small children were led outside
and dispersed across the plain
where Mongol horsemen galloped about
spearing them and trampling them.
Timur Beg finally set fire to Ispahan
and departed for his capital
which was called Semerchant, or
as some pronounce it, Samarkand.
Compared to this, considering our purpose,
how could anybody claim we've done wrong?
Quae caret ora cruore nost...

My son whispers that he intends to leave;
friends tell him it's possible to escape
and find refuge in Canada. God Speed, I say.

Montesquieu warns that we must be truthful
in all things, even if they concern our country.

We offer solatium—that is, compensation or solace
in the form of money to the relatives of civilians
killed by our soldiers. The value we've established
for one Vietnamese is 4,000 *piasters*, equal to $14.55.

The Commandant of Fort Detrick, Colonel Gershater,
remarks that children frequently come to visit
the Animal Farm, as it's called, where guinea pigs,
mice, hamsters and monkeys are used in experiments
with viruses. Human volunteers for these tests
are picked from two categories: criminals, and those
who refuse to fight in Vietnam. Is this a German dream?

Montagnard peasants whose crops have been poisoned
in the herbicidal program may apply for compensation
by properly completing not 1 or 2 or 3, but 9 copies
of the appropriate form. This speaks for itself.

Successful implementation of America's recent proposal
for the highland provinces of Quang Ngai and Qyang Tin
calls for the destruction of 15,000 metric tons of food.
Would you care to comment?

My brother-in-law's face magically metamorphoses
into wood if certain ugly subjects are discussed.
He reminds me of the Puritan divine, Cotton Mather,
righteously declaring after an epidemic decimated
every Indian village from Maine to Rhode Island
that God swept the forest of pernicious creatures
to make room for a better growth.

Lord Amherst, outraged by violations of European law,
instructed the commandant of a punitive expedition
to regard the Seneca "not as a generous enemy
but as the vilest race of beings that ever infested
the earth, and whose riddance from it may be esteemed
as a meritorious act, for the good of mankind."

Accordingly, no prisoners were taken; every savage
encountered was killed at the first opportunity.
Plus ça change, plus c'est la même, say the French,
implying how little we change.

Kentucky frontiersmen who found the body of Tecumseh
sliced off strips of his skin to use as razor strops.

After the Indian leader Philip had been shot
Captain Church ordered his body quartered
and sent his head to Plymouth where it hung on a gibbet
for 20 years. One of his hands was sent to Boston
as a curiosity.

Captain Simeon Ecuyer, besieged at Fort Pitt
by a war party of Mingo, Shawnee and Delaware,
sent the Indians a gift consisting of two blankets
and a handkerchief from the smallpox hospital.
Does this remind you of anything?

So many generals marched up and down Florida
chasing Seminoles, and the collapse of resistance
was announced by the Army with such regularity
that it became embarrassing. *Plus ça change,* etc.

If I sound blunt, I apologize. But a senseless order
rules the affairs of men, leaving us little choice;
all we can do is enlarge the indictment. Into this journal
goes "Nixon" because of unspeakable pretense, deceit
and deliberate savagery.

Wilfrid Owen was killed just a week before the Armistice.
A poet who held much for the future of English literature,
courageous enough as courage goes—rebegot like Donne
of absence and darkness—what was his death worth?

People like to say that if Dante, Petrarch, Chaucer,
Boccaccio, Calderón, Lord Bacon, Shakespeare and Milton
had never lived we would experience worse wars, usury,
more oppressive fraud, malfeasance and servitude.

I doubt it. I think they functioned as entertainers
who taught nothing. I submit that the continuation
of everything they abhorred substantiates my argument.

Whether Good or Evil ultimately triumphs
I don't presume to know; but so much we condemn
glitters like a rising star.

I heard our President's latest address to the nation
and thought of the Inquisition's fundamental philosophy
holding that Error has no rights. Tell me, friend,
what century is this?

Why does the Devil attend school?
To study foreign languages.
Where are the marks of His talons?
*On the wall of the south porch
of the Church of Saint Pancr...*

Remember, great civilizations require
mighty antagonists.

Parallels persist. Innocent III offered absolution
from all sins past, present and future to those
who would destroy the Albigensian heresy. Who's next?

Mahometans and Jews believe there's no dogma
as susceptible to the blasphemies of heretics
and the mockeries of politicians as Christianity.
How, they inquire, can God be eaten in bread?
Behold! a people that feeds upon its deity!
Flies and worms could subsist on His carcass!

Opportunities for ridicule are endless.
Saint Macaire undertook 7 years' penance
among a forest of brambles for killing a louse.

Saint Simeon Stylites stood on one foot for a year;
his body turned into a mass of ulcers.

Surely we must be children of fantastic dreams
who might say with Richardus de Sancto Victore
upon the Day of Judgment: *Lord, if we be deceived
thou alone has deceived us.*

You may know, or you may not: Jesus of Nazareth
was celebrated as an exorcist, healing many
who had been invaded by devils, along with lunatics
and those suffering from palsy. At Capernum
he recorded his most significant success
when he compelled a spirit to leave a demoniac.
If this sounds odd you need only to remind yourself
that God and Satan, like Siamese twins,
are so joined that they can never be separated.
Death for one means death for the other.
Differently expressed: *Manus manum lavat.*

By accepting the miracles of Christianity
we reject the great miracle of alchemy,
whose apparent purpose—the transmutation
of metal—is of less concern to adepts
that the transmutation of a human soul.
Zosimus the Panopolitan puts it like this:
*He who looks in a mirror looks not at shadows
but at what the shadows hint, understanding
reality through fictitious appearances.*

Regarding the origin of Alchemy, opinions differ.
The word probably comes from the Arabic *alkimia*
which some say derived from the Egyptians' name
for their country—that being *kmt* or *chem*,
black land, referring to the Nile's alluvial soil
as opposed to tawny desert sand, for this art
flourished in Nilotic Egypt. On the other hand
kmt or *chem* is never used in ancient texts
to define alchemy. Perhaps the word *chyma*,
which is a Greek word meaning to fuse metal,
is its root. In any case, during the Middle Ages
a majority of alchemical adepts were Muslim
and many of them were strangled while they slept
on the assumption, justifiable or not,

that they possessed the Philosopher's Stone,
which has been sought by m en of every age.

Azoth, the mercury of philosophers,
comes from *al-zāūq*. Its occult power
is prodigious, containing as it does
the first and last letters of the Greek,
Roman, Arabic and Hebrew alphabets.

The alkahest, being a universal solvent,
must by definition dissolve any vessel
into which it is poured, as was pointed out
by Kunckel. He thinks its name may derive from
alkali est, the meaning of which is obvious;
or from the German *All-Geist*, universal spirit;
or possibly *All ist*, it is all. However,
he doubts if any such dissolvent could exist
and refers to it with unmistakable contempt
as *Alles Lugen ist*. In other words, it's a lie.

In every so-called "transmutation" a skeptical mind
sooner or later perceives where the charlatan acted,
except for one notable demonstration performed
by the celebrated Helvetius during January of 1666.
In this case, fearing that he had been deceived
by a mysterious stranger who gave him, as a favor,
a metallic crumb—because Helvetius himself
was profoundly suspicious of alchemical boasts—
this respected man in the presence of his wife
and several witnesses added the magic crumb
to a crucible containing 6 drams of old lead.
And within a quarter of an hour, he reports,
it had been transmuted into the purest gold,
which astonished not only himself and his wife
but everybody else. Carrying the aurified lead,
still hot, Helvetius hurried to a nearby goldsmith
who marveled at its fineness and offered 50 florins
to the ounce. Now you probably doubt the story,
but I don't. If you should ask why, I'd repeat
out of the eminent pragmatism of an age: *Credo
quia absurdum est.*

Here's a story about the Swedish General Paykhull.
Convicted of treason and sentenced to death,
he volunteers to make a million crowns of gold
annually, swearing he'd been taught the secret
of transmutation from a Pole who had obtained it
from a Corinthian priest. King Charles was dubious
but our true king is Avarice. A test was arranged,
supervised by a British officer named Hamilton
of the Royal Artillery. Precautions against fraud
were either useless or unnecessary—at this date
how do we know? All we can establish is that
as a result of General Paykhull's demonstration
Charles got a huge lump of gold which he coined
into 147 ducats; and he ordered a medallion struck
giving the general's name, the place and date.
This occurred in the city of Stockholm in 1706.
About Paykhull himself—well, he disappeared.
What's left are a few of the ducats, his medallion
and the likelihood that he won a desperate bet.
Fortunes, as you see, are various.

Domenico Manuel Caetano, a Neapolitan peasant
apprenticed to a goldsmith, having learnt conjuring
and having practiced enough to satisfy himself,
announced that he had found an ancient manuscript
which described how to prepare the Philosopher's Stone.
Because of some apparently successful transmutations
he was invited by the Bavarian ambassador in Madrid
to prove his ability before Maximilian Emanuel,
Governor of the Spanish Netherlands in Brussels.
Successful again, he was awarded 60,000 *gulden*;
but when he attempted to get out of the country
official suspicions flowered like tulips. Caught,
tried and convicted, Domenico was jailed for 6 years.
Later he turned up in Vienna where he amazed everybody,
including Emperor Leopold the First. Then to Berlin
where he promised to prepare a quantity of the stone
within 60 days in exchange for all sorts of gifts
and a lucrative office. But there was a little trouble
and having observed that the king was growing restless

Domenico decided to leave. He was captured in Hamburg
and dropped into the fortress of Küstrin. Complaining
that nobody could vindicate himself in such a place
he was allowed to return to Berlin, and before long
he tried once more to escape. Well, enough's enough.
In August of that year, 1709, resplendently dressed
in a cloak spangled with tinsel Domenico Manuel Caetano
reluctantly went dancing beneath a gilded gallows.
As bold as a Swedish general, he proved less adroit
—which sometimes calls the coin.

Are we not of a thousand kinds,
diverse as the colors of our lives?
Mille hominum species et rerum
discolor usus; velle suum
cuique est, nec voto vivitur uno.

Albertus Magnus, Doctor Universalis,
Count of Bollstädt, who offered fragments of iron
to ostriches and welcomed the fabulous,
was born at Lauingen in Suabia
probably around 1493, and as a young man
joined the Dominican Order at Padua.
Later he taught at Freiburg, Ratisbon,
Cologne and Strasburg, gave lectures in Paris,
eventually became Provincial of his Order
and in good time was appointed Bishop of Ratisbon
—but left his luxurious episcopal palace
in favor of a cloister where he meditated,
studied and wrote for the rest of his life
because the duties of a prominent ecclesiastic
seemed to him less flattering than onerous.
We could use more such men.

Adelard of Bath was another good man. Although
neither his birth date nor that of his death
can be verified, we know he studied at Tours
and Laon, and traveled through Africa, Italy
and Asia Minor before returning to England.
There, when he inquired about the state of things,

he was told that the princes were jealous
and violent, the prelates drunkards, the judges
corrupt, patrons inconstant, men who made promises
played false, and everyone had grown ambitious.
Then a nephew of Adelard, noticing his uncle's
distress, said if he was offended by such depravity
he had best write a book describing his travels
and include for the English public's benefit
as much as he had learned. This is what Adelard did,
being a conscientious man. I've studied his book
and I don't mind telling you we agree on most matters.

Of course I've gone farther than Adelard.
I've been to places he never imagined.
I went with Sindbad to the court of the King
of Sarandib, who gave him a ruby a span high
and a bed covered with the skin of a serpent
that had swallowed a full-grown elephant,
and a slave girl like a shining moon.
Now, my friend, what do you say to that?

I've never had children, or married,
but I've been the spectator many times
while other lives played. Adventures,
vast fortunes—nothing startles me.
I've beheld a universe present itself:
meteors, prodigies, grievances, funerals,
martyrs, sea battles, apparitions,
massacres, heresies, schisms, vows,
proclamations, monomachies, mummeries,
stratagems, weddings, embassies,
wishes. Unwillingly when the time comes
I'll cede my box at such a theater.

Listen. I saw King John of England
on his deathbed, disguised as a monk
to avoid the tortures of Hell;
Bajazet, caged by Tamerlane
and exhibited like a beast,
beating his brains against the bars.

I've heard the nightingale, my friend,
noted a few lucky days with chalk
like a Roman, climbed the great mastabah
of Imhotep, counted Atahualpa's ransom
which filled a room at Cajamarca with silver
as high as a man could reach.

I've talked with Friar Odoric
who was entertained at a banquet
in the palace of the Khan,
who spoke of golden peacocks
spreading their wings
and drawing up their trains
whenever the Khan clapped his hands.

I've tasted spices from forgotten islands;
smelled the fragrance of Gul-i-Mazar,
flower of the graves, that blooms
where the last Arab prince of Granada
was laid to rest.

With Fidelis I've made a pilgrimage to Jerusalem
down a canal connecting the Red Sea with the Nile,
sailing four days from one end to the other;
I've visited Glastonbury Tor, the renowned isle
of Avalon, where King Arthur lies waiting
to rescue the world from heathen savagery
and wicked men—not far from Pomparlès,
that perilous bridge across the Brue
were Excalibur was cast into the water.

I know the location of Buddha's footprints.
Three of the four I've seen; and by tomorrow
if the wind holds we'll raise the Ceylon coast.

You ask who I am.
How could I tell you
if you don't already know?
Let's say I make butterflies
—butterflies of song,

only to release them.
Ça suffice?

Listen. I'm a Clerk of the King's Works
in charge of docks, sewers, walls
and bridges. When I have time I translate
Boethius, write poems or amend my treatise
concerning the astrolabe. If you're a scholar
you've spotted me as Geoffrey Chaucer.

Charged with treason by Theodoric,
waiting untried to be put to death,
without haste I compose my testament:
The Consolation of Philosophy.
A member of high Roman nobility,
my name is Anicius Manlius Sev . . .

I've deceived you again! The fact is,
since I went blind my hours are spent
teaching three ignorant daughters
to pronounce the words of six languages
so they can feed me with knowledge.
As for my name, what's the difference?
Say I'm John Milton, if you like.

Look, the use of a man's name
among the Masai brings bad luck;
if you want to know what he's called
you'd just better ask somebody else.
As for my purpose, there's no mystery.
I'm attempting to do what Nature does;
that is, to set people dreaming.

In the celestial city of Machu Picchu
the Incas studied earthquakes, rainbows,
the flight of birds and the dung of animals.
I follow their example.

Frequently I turn to Sir Thomas Browne
for the most intricate and elaborate English
conceivable. Having apprenticed myself,

I find that I am able to comment, criticize
and persevere. This gentleman's lessons
are invaluable, believe me.

Saint-Beuve's critical articles fill 48 volumes,
but I have 500 planned.

Carlyle extolled the virtues of silence
in 19 volumes. Myself, I'm talkative.
I think we have so much to communicate
that I'd punish taciturn people.

I have a neighbor who's an Astrophysicist.
When I asked about the Riemann-Christoffel tensor
he remarked that an elementary explanation
would necessitate the genius of a Langevin
as well as the pages of a ponderous volume,
but even then I might be puzzled.
Was ich nicht weiss, macht mich nicht heiss,
I told him and walked away.

I take a simple view of things.
I think the world has substance and quality,
intellect feeding on itself is poisonous,
and most meanings sink into our senses
without assistance.

When I visited the laboratory of my cousin
the Anatomist, he showed me some pineal tissue
which he said was the remnant of a third eye
within the skull that originally looked up
to notify the brain of shadows passing overhead
while we slept. I was impressed by this;
often I think about it.

I've heard that a computer equivalent in strength
to a human brain might be as small as a matchbox,
but what technician could create a sphere so deft,
marvelous and unique?

What computer is able to distinguish between
l'esprit de géométrie, the deductive argument
of a scholar or scientist, and *l'esprit de finesse*
which is the power of intuition? After all,
emotion has a logic incomprehensible to reason.

Michelson, for example, relied upon intuition
while formulating an equation for tidal phenomena
and when a mathematician reported incongruous data
he rejected it, predicating a mathematical error
which was finally located.

Poincaré speaks of leaving Caen where he lived
in order to go on a geological expedition
under the auspices of the School of Mines.
This caused him temporarily to forget his work,
but after the group had stopped at Coutances
and he was climbing aboard the bus—just as he
touched the step with his foot it occurred to him
that arithmetic transformations of indeterminate
ternary quadratic forms were identical with
those of non-Euclidean geometry. At the moment
he made no attempt to verify his intuition;
all he did was to take a seat in the bus
and continue a geological conversation.
But he tells us he had no doubt about it.
Later, at Caen, the hypothesis was proved.

Lord Russell, wandering toward the university
capriciously tossing a tin of pipe tobacco
and catching it, perceived at the exact instant
a ray of sunlight glinted from the metal surface
that the ontological argument was sound.

Stravinsky, it's said, never once paused
to justify his diatonic methods, relying instead
on the intelligence of his inner ear.

What all of this means is that we can profit
from studying the lives of exceptional men

because they seldom forget a truth embodied
by the Greeks in this phrase: *Gnothi seauton*.
Not that their richest ideas are acclaimed
at once; sometimes genius is met with silence.
Eight years of indifference greeted Einstein's
germinal document. Not one scientist responded.
Not one. It's hard to believe.

In 1676, having studied Jupiter's satellites,
Alaus Roemer concluded that the instantaneous
propagation of light was a scientific mistake;
yet orthodox convictions proved so persuasive
that his hypothesis was ignored for fifty years.

Grotefend deciphered Persepolitan cuneiform script
and set forth his conclusions in three reports.
Who knows why this startling research was neglected?

Waldeck's account of Palenque lay unpublished until 1866,
the year he celebrated his 100th birthday.

Francis Bacon, having expropriated all known facts,
anticipated Newton's law by more than half a century.
What did it get him? Dust and shadow. The remembrance
of mastered difficulties, I'm told, tastes sweet. Perhaps.

Great men are born out of joint as often as not.
Nostradamus never wondered about people flying;
such sights were common in his prophetic visions.
At the University of Montpellier he got his doctorate
with extraordinary speed and became a physician
who cured hundreds of people by unorthodox remedies,
for which he was slandered and vilified.

Priestley was driven out of England
by the rage of conservatives
because he analyzed the air we breathe.

When news got about that Wilhelm Roentgen
had photographed the bones in his wife's hand

modest women refused to leave their houses,
fearful of men with X-ray eyes, and bankers
struggled with panic, afraid that the contents
of their vaults would be revealed. Roentgen,
Roentgen, Roentgen—that was all you heard!
He was a wizard, maybe the most dangerous
who ever lived, etc. Fortunately, appearance
passes and truth abides. *Schein vergeht,*
Wahrheit bes . . .

My wife just walked by holding her nose.
Haven't changed your shirt in three weeks!
she cries. Look at the chocolate on your beard!
and so forth. She mimics my long scooping stride,
refers to me as her dedicated little hunchback,
although my hump is what first attracted her.
Later is was my brain, of course, but at present
only our habits bind us. A man's dearest quality,
she likes to say, hoping I'll feel humiliated,
is self-control. *Opse theon aleousi myloi aleousi*
de lepta, I answer, knowing she can't understand.
Not after all these years.

I imagine my wife's heart resembles the organ of a fish.
And how sick I've gotten of her milky translucence.
Heated baths, towels, oils, night after night my sleep
disturbed by unnatural requests. Sooner or later, though,
everything passes, all vanishes, the heart forgets.

In April of 1485 some workmen who were quarrying marble
along the Via Appia near the 6th milestone outside Rome
happened to break through a vault and found a sarcophagus
containing a girl's body thickly coated with an unfamiliar
fragrant greasy substance. Except for a slight flattening
of her loins and breast she seemed untouched by death.
Her black hair had been arranged in a maidenly knot
and was covered with an elaborate snood of silk and gold.
Her teeth were small and perfect and remarkably white;
her subtly parted lips yielded easily to pressure.
Her tongue retained the color and flexibility of life

and her supple limbs could be lifted or rearranged
into almost any position. The sarcophagus was examined
for inscriptions, but not a word was found anywhere;
and if originally there was a monument above her tomb
it had long since disintegrated or had been removed.
Nothing else could be learned about the mysterious girl
because Pope Innocent VIII, shocked and horrified
by a specter so closely simulating life, ordered her body
carried in the middle of the night to a deserted area
beyond the Porta Pinciana where it was secretly reburied.

A boy amusing himself with a rake in the Alcudia de Elche
near Murcia uncovered the sculpted head of a woman
whose intricate coiffure suggested the Spanish comb
but whose breast was adorned with Phoenician amulets.
Some laborers in a field who were the first to see her,
astounded by her beauty, called her The Moorish Queen.
But whether she represented an actual woman or a deity,
perhaps an influential priestess of the Punic god Thanit,
has never been determined.

Contradictory images plead for our attention;
memories of love long past persist. An ivory figure
of Lakshmi, Vishnu's consort and Goddess of Love,
was excavated at Pompeii.

In the Musée Guimet a little Egyptian girl stands waiting,
her last bouquet clasped in leathery arms.

On the Riviera near Antibes a Roman tombstone
with a Latin inscription tells us that a visitor
from the North, aged 12, danced and gave pleasure.

R-K1.
Q-B2.

The heart engages itself in a bitter struggle
with the body's other parts, so I've heard.
Perhaps this is true—though personally
I haven't been aware of any conflict.

I've neither offered love nor accepted it;
men and women look pretty much the same.
Why? I suspect because of my elderly parents
who tied my hands at night when I was a child.
The inevitable result is that I've abstained
from every sort of pleasurable human intercourse.
I suppose I should feel deprived, but I don't.
If you contrast solitude's uninterrupted satisfaction
with those senseless male and female paroxysms
you'll see what I mean.

Friends say I have about me a peculiar lassitude
which causes me to remain oblivious to everything;
they say I'm sunk in putrescent indolence. I tell them
about a microscopist who descried a woman in a waterdrop
and fell in love with her and spent his life observing.
Some people immediately understand, others are baffled.
To the obtuse I say nothing else; I merely point out
Hieronymus Bosch's terrifying *Garden of Earthly Delights*
where gigantic strawberries symbolize human impermanence.

Now and then, I admit, I wonder why I was denied
what others seem to regard as a natural privilege;
but before long I forget, succumbing to fabulous voyages.

Lat. 61.13 N.; Long. 30.08 W.
Currents flow, the needle turns north
by northwest. Last night it pointed
due south. What makes it vary?
The Pole Star? A lodestone?
The nearness of a new continent?
Situated in a vein of the earth
is there a magnetical meridian?
If you can tell me, my friend,
you're more sapient than Maurolicus,
Scaliger, Agricola, Cortesius
and the Coimbrians.

Fabatus considers seafaring men mad
because the waters of the sea are mad,

they never stand still; because the ship
must be mad to remain in constant motion;
because the wind is mad if it has no idea
whence it came or whither it will fly.
So mariners exposing themselves to madness
must be mad.

Imagine, as philosophers postulate,
that the earth is another moon:
then we're all lunatic and vertiginous
within a sublunary maze. Can you doubt it?

One of my countrymen fell into a pit of frogs,
swallowed some water and soon became convinced
he'd swallowed frog's spawn, and after a while
claimed to feel frogs moving in his belly
fed by his juices, and spent seven full years
wandering through Europe consulting physicians.
And being told it was his own wind and conceit
he attempted to contradict the doctors
by maintaining it was not wind but frogs,
and said they were deaf not to hear the croaks.
You're ignorant if you take this for a joke.
Mit der Dummheit kämpfen Götter selbst vergebens.

Some avow that we spring from mushrooms
and keep our wits in jars. I think so,
as I watch what happens.

Do metals grow in the bowels of the earth?
Where are the 4,000 cities of ancient Egypt?

Where do birds go when it's cold?
They abandon Muscovy during winter,
yet in spring the hedges creak and rustle.
Have they been asleep like alpine mice,
or do they lie at the bottom of lakes
holding their breath? So they're found
by fishermen of Scandia and Poland
two together, mouth to mouth, wing to wing.

Perhaps they follow the sun to Africa.
Whence they come, whither they migrate
we know not. The same's true of questions.

How far is it from the tongue to the penis?
Caesar's troops, we're told, bawled obscene songs
in accentual meters. *Qualis artifex pereo.*

The poet Lucretius was driven mad by a love philter:
what wounds the mind with love, the body seeks.

Socrates, speaking of love, concealed his face;
but that's not uncommon.

Spallanzani, studying the embrace of toads,
found out that in spite of decapitation
the male continued clinging to the female.

Now I'll tell you about the anatomist Vesalius.
Performing an autopsy on the body of a patient
whose inexplicable death troubled him
Vesalius dissected the rib cage of the corpse
only to discover a living, palpitating heart.

A similar lust for knowledge overtook King James IV
of Scotland, who left two foundlings with a mute woman
on Inchkeith Island and ordered her to raise them
because he wanted to hear what language they'd speak.
The result of the King's experiment has been lost,
which is too bad. According to legend, the foundlings
spoke perfect Hebrew; but just why this should be
nobody seems to know.

An instructive experiment was conducted in Denmark
by several doctors who were given a condemned prisoner.
First, they blindfolded him. Next, slight incisions
were made in his arms and legs and four water taps
near the operating table were turned on. Regrettably
the victim died of terror before they could finish.

Many think the apex of human arrogance was Paracelsus
who prophesied that the time would come when a voice
might travel 100 miles by the aid of pipes or crystals.
Well, you say, who could imagine anything so absurd!
It's all the more curious because he was an erudite man,
author of an ambitious book: *Sagacious Philosophy
of the Great and Small World*, 397 pages in length,
a compendium of superstitions and beliefs, occult
sciences, salvation and related matters, chiromantics,
pyromantics, characterism, signatures, phrenology,
physiognomy, astrology, geometry, the healing power
of stones, algorithm, cosmography, sorcerers, ghosts,
witches, meteorology and technology. For all that,
according to his amanuensis, this celebrated magus
often mumbled to himself for hours, spent much time
in front of an oven concocting stinking powders,
grew angry without cause, yelped, threw fits, fought
with friends and rejected everybody who tried to help him.
It's believed he died from an overdose of a thaumaturgic
elixir he carried in the pommel of his sword, although
some scholars say he was killed during a tavern quarrel.
At any rate, after his death his pathetic loneliness
was revealed by the fact that not one of his manuscripts
had been bequeathed to anybody. Evidently he'd never met
a person he liked and trusted. *Athanasius contra mundum*,
so to speak; and we perpetuate his name neither for his
predictions nor for his eccentricities but for his relentless
struggle against orthodoxy.

Together, Paracelsus and the Augustinian monk
Luther represent cuttings from a single stem:
German peasants, knotty, pugnacious and devout,
less attentive to illiberal canons of authority
than to an inner voice. *Du bist am Ende was du bist.*

Now let me tell you about the swastika
which has been utilized so many places
at so many times. Ever since the Bronze Age
it has appeared on crematory urns,
as though linked to fire. In East Anglia

we find it on vases, in Saxon England
and in the north countries on sword hilts.
It seems to be a lucky and protective sign
associated with the harsh Norse god Woden.
What I'm trying to say is that the Nazis
in their effort to revive a cult of fanatical
devotion must have felt a very deep affinity
for this ominous hooked cross.

In German orphanages before each meal
the following prayer is offered:
To Thee alone I owe my daily bread;
abandon thou me never, with me forever
abide, Fuehrer, my Fuehrer, my Faith . . .

That its wars are defensive is the myth of every nation.
Let's listen to the American general, Douglas MacArthur:
A warlike spirit, which alone can create and civilize a state,
is absolutely essential to national defense and to national . . .
But why continue? He goes on to admonish us that each male
brought into existence should be instructed from earliest
infancy that honor and distinction march side by side
with military service, and his life should be permeated
by the ideal that death becomes a boon if one dies
fulfilling his country's destiny.

It is the Anglo-Saxon manifest destiny
to go forth in the world as a world conqueror.
He will take possession of all the islands of the sea.
He will exterminate the people he cannot subjugate.
That is what fate holds for the chosen people.
Can you guess who wrote that? Does it matter?

Destiny beckons America to hold and civilize Mexico,
says Secretary of State Buchanan. Is he correct?

Here's the Nashville *Clarion* advocating
the annexation of a neighbor or two:
Where is it written in the book of fate
that the American republic shall not stretch

from the Chesapeake capes to Nootka Sound,
from the Isthmus of Panama to Huds . . .

But I expect you'd be more interested to learn that
a single cubic inch of Procyon B weighs 200 tons,
and Rigel is 32,400 times as brilliant as the sun.
I could unroll a tapestry of exemplary actions
to impress you, or amuse you with miscellaneous
oddities, such as the fact that Darwin spent hours
measuring the exact speed of Galapagos tortoises
and Herodotus believed the Ethiop's generative seed
to be as black as ink. Let me know which you prefer.

Possibly you'd like to be told about the Kaffir
who have 26 terms to differentiate the color markings
of cattle, or hear stories told by Mexican chicle hunters
of ancient Mayan temples they've come across accidentally
while looking for the sapodilla tree, which is our source
of chewing gum.

Did you know that travel is marvelously sustaining?
It is, but so is the meat of gelded camels.

Has anybody told you that birds travel in flocks
to confuse hawks?
The same's true of women's speech.

Are you aware that astrologers proliferate
and swarm out of their caves like bats
whenever our fear of war increases?
Do you know about Kuniyoshi's wish
to paint a dark object within the dark?

Have you heard that Nero enjoyed gladiatorial performances
through optical glasses? Indeed he did.

Here's something else. In flamboyant medieval Spain
those wretched heretics about to be publicly toasted
were often dressed up in a dalmatic and crowned
with a bishop's miter. By the way, inquisitorial familiars

weren't affected by their victims' groans and shrieks;
what was done was being done, they felt, for the person's
benefit. Whether or not you agree, God knows.

If we search for ecclesiastics our Maker blessed
with some sensibility we encounter almost at once
St. Ignatius Loyola, who confesses that in fact
he actually enjoyed his profane thoughts—although
subsequently experiencing desiccation and discontent.

If we set ourselves to identify a few secular brothers
whose ethical nature staggers us, we find it difficult
to forget Johnson's zealous lieutenants. Mark them
until a new Nuremberg comes riding down the wind.

Congressman Gerald Ford urges the impeachment
of Supreme Court Justice William O. Douglas.
Tomorrow or tomorrow neither name will mean much;
nevertheless, I list them because they constitute
opposing fragments of a humanity's stupendous mosaic.
Maybe I could express this a bit more succinctly:
Fruitful and poisonous blossoms intermingle.

I realize I don't always make my position clear.
Let's try again. There were omens when Baldar fell
and the gods dreamed murderous dreams.

No, wait. Civilization, so precariously erected,
may be destroyed by the forces we conceal.

I suppose it could be said another way:
into the pattern of human events
God weaves misfortune
so that each generation shall find a song to sing.

Did you speak?
Come a little closer,
take my hand.
Who am I?
Call me a singer:

Sing goddamm,
damm,
sing Goddamm.

All day my uncle wanders back and forth
in his robe and carpet slippers. He sighs,
explaining what he might have accomplished
if he'd been a film actor or a statesman,
if he'd not felt so obligated to his wife
and to the high authority of his office
or the responsibility of a walnut dining table.
If I'd just had a bit of luck, he mutters.
But as you know by now, where the heart leads
we follow. *Dhia Bith leat chun an ath . . .*

I feel lethargic, unable to concentrate.
I'm filled with doubts that puzzle the doctors.
I have trouble recalling my name; in the mirror
I observe the face of a man I used to know.
I'm able to see footprints before making them,
fatal words occur to me as they did to Caedmon.
Perhaps something is generated in each of us
which before trial we seek, but having tried
eschew. We so earnestly wish and covet much
and eftsoons grow weary.

I remember a man in Calcutta who followed me
all night; what he wanted I never understood,
but wherever I turned I met his furious eyes.

Passions of a thousand kinds, rage and jealousy
overwhelm us.

I guess we dream of what we desire, like Sarmiento
commanded to go and chart the Straits of Magellan
by the Prorex of Peru; and standing on a mountaintop
was sure he descried a beautiful country gleaming
with towers, monuments and temples past counting
—greater than the greatest masterworks of Europe.

As deluded as Sarmiento, if less than Pythagoras
vainly trying to read inscriptions on the moon,
our President thought he could see the heart of Asia.
Ex umbris et imaginibus . . .

Madmen, like those near death, according to Galen,
hold in their eyes images of what they think they see.

Here's how the *Encyclopédie* defines madness:
"to depart from reason with confidence
in the conviction that one is following it."
Not many influential people escape this net.
Bishop Gislebert of Lisieux, for instance,
interpreted meteorites showering across Europe
in April of 1095 as a signal from God
calling for a militant invasion of the East.

Goethe wasted months wandering through Sicily
looking for the *Urpflanze*, an ideal plant
from which all other plants have degenerated
as a result of various unfavorable influences.

George Washington employed a curious device
consisting of two rods three inches long,
known as Perkins' Patented Metal Tractor,
to draw unspecified diseases out of his body.

André Pujom, realizing that the anagram *Pendu à Riom*
could be made of his name, committed a capital offense
for which he was convicted and subsequently hanged
at Riom, just as he anticipated. Does madness ever end?

Does madness end? Well, suppose we put it like this:
Troubled by a suit of law they were unable to resolve,
the Areopagites ordered the contending parties to leave
and return for a decision in 100 years.

Robert Piere, awaiting execution at San Quentin prison,
contrived to slash his throat with a shard of glass,
precipitating a frantic quarrel among the authorities:

some insisted that he be executed before he bled to death
while others thought he should be taken to the hospital.
Presently, with gouts of blood bubbling from his neck,
he was carried into the gas chamber. Witnesses screamed,
vomited and several fainted. The decision had been reached,
officials later explained, because at the time of death
the prisoner probably would still be alive and therefore
conscious not only of his crime but of the retribution
justly demanded by the Sovereign State of California.
I've twice asked the question; if you know the answer
tell me.

Listen. You might find this procedure edifying:
16 pellets of cyanide in a gauze bag are suspended
from a hook beneath the chair. A gallon of distilled
water is mixed with sulphuric acid in a jar,
which is connected by a tube to a shallow pan
just under the seat. The prisoner, a stethoscope
taped to his chest, assisted by two guards
—ah well, enough's enough. The madness of one
can drive many mad. *Unius dementia, etc.*

That emotional discharge known to analysts
and to the earliest Greeks as *katharsis*
seems increasingly difficult to achieve;
obsessed with doubt, submerged by ritual
we miss the clean freehand slash of a blade.

The sense of sin relates more intimately
to inhibition than to indulgence, I'm told,
and the exquisite conscience suffers most.
Maybe. But whose opinion should we trust?

Pater nost...

Father, I said, is perfection obligatory?
My son, he answered, this is Good Friday.

Father, I said, polite euphemisms I despise
and facetious circumlocutions I deplore.

The God that holds you over the pit of Hell,
he said, much as one might hold a spider
or some loathsome object over a fire
abhors you and is dreadfully provoked.

Father, I said, estranged from the current of my nation
how should I live? The Knights Templars of the Crusades
were esteemed, he said, not only for their military skills
but as bankers.

Father, I said, is it true that war is at the same time
painful and deeply desired? To be in battle, my son,
is to be in harmony with the rhythm of the universe.

Father, I said, whenever I hear of a new catastrophe
in southeast Asia I'm reminded of British grenadiers
struggling like automatons through our Louisiana swamps.
The Grandee possesses an ability to calculate ten moves
in advance, he said. The Proxime's vision is less.
Would you care for a game?

P-K5.
N-Q2.

Father, I said, is it not unholy and terrible
to boast about slain men? Among the oldest words
in our language, he said, are "hammer" and "sickle"
which have been employed since the Stone Age.
He smiled, scratched his head and continued:
It is easy to combat the prejudices of others,
I quite enjoy that. But to fight against my own
is both impossible and disagreeable. Therefore
I baptize thee not in the name of the Father
but in the name of the Devil. It's six o'clock.
Suppose we tune in the news.

A Protestant voice extrudes:
Communist troops ambushed this morning
at Quang Tri suffered heavy cas . . .

The bodies of enemy Vietnamese are arranged in rows
so as to present a symmetrical soldierly appearance
when inspected by reporters and Congressional officials.
Later they are sprayed with lime from a white bin
slung like an incense burner beneath the fuselage
of a Chinook helicopter, despite Lieutenant General
Burley's conviction that corpses should be left to rot
in the fields as an example to potential sympathizers.
Well, satisfaction adopts many masks and to each
his own. In the words of Vergil: *Trahit sua quemque
voluptas.*

A moment ago my mother stopped by the bed to ask
how I was feeling. I told her about Francisco José
de Goya y Lucientes drawing *Los Caprichos* from memory,
gathering dreams to record, and horrifying fantasies
and criticism of the world. I doubt if she understood
but I hope you do. Nothing else matters.

Look, I'm writing a gnomic book about America
because not long ago when the entrails of an eagle
were studied for fatidic signs a vile odor spread
and the heart was found misplaced. Now tell me
—oh, never mind. It won't make any difference.

Sunday. Easter Sunday. Happy Easter to you! God bless!
The Venerable Bede informs us that the word's derived
from *Eastre*, goddess of springtime in the pagan pantheon
of our forefathers. Others say it's an English term
which means "rising." Regardless of the etymology
this day signifies a dawning. And so, by extension,
it means the resurrection of a compassionate savior.

Gilded eggs were exchanged by Egyptians
during the new moon in April, honoring Osiris
who was murdered but subsequently resurrected.
So you see the genesis of a Christian ritual;
once a year we give our children blood-red tokens
of an unpleasant Nilotic legend.

For the origin of Christmas
we look to the Roman saturnalia.
Eh? You say you know that? Hmm!
Do you know about Saint Nicholas?
Listen. In the village of Patara
in Asia Minor during Diocletian's reign
lived a very old man with three daughters
for whom he was unable to provide a dowry.
The girls were ready to prostitute themselves
when the good bishop of Myra, Nicholas,
secretly left a bag of gold in their house.
Because of his generosity we celebrate
a corruption of the kindly bishop's name,
a bizarre caricature called Santa Claus.

Could you guess the genesis of the wedding ring?
Mesopotamian cylinder seals were altered by Egyptians
into the shape of a ring with the sacred horned beetle,
or scarab, carved on top and some personal design
incised on the undersurface. So, if a ring was reversed
it would serve very nicely as a seal of ownership;
and a man who placed one on his wife's hand
signified that he was entrusting to her custody
all of his possessions. In other words, it symbolizes
not bondage as we commonly suppose, but absolute trust.

You're familiar, of course, with the *couvade*
in which men and women act alike during childbirth.
What you may have forgotten is that it recalls to us
our androgynous beginning when both sexes yielded milk.

Superstition, plethora of custom, vestiges and relics
combine and juxtapose to persuade society of its past
just as I surround myself with fragments of previous
civilizations: pottery, disintegrating jade beads,
splintered wooden puppets, textiles, totems, discovered
artifacts of half-buried cultures. Nothing's too small
or fragile; not much eludes my delicate grasp.

On my bookcase rests a splendid cylindrical Mayan bowl
made by some anonymous craftsman 10 or 11 centuries ago
near Puebla. Although the glaze has nearly disappeared
it's still possible to make out a diagonal orange stripe
beneath the glyphs. I liken it to an ambassador's ribbon;
to my nephew this band suggests an oblique fascistic stripe
on the waistcoat of the United States—which seems to me
ridiculous and implausible, a characteristic excess of youth.
I admit, however, that he and his friends do seem to be right
occasionally.

Mayan civilization lasted 3,000 years more or less,
depending on how the evidence is interpreted.
As to the duration of our Judeo-Christian world,
we might anticipate another 5 or 6 centuries;
to look beyond that would be presumptuous.

If you wander through the tombs at Cerveteri
among those obese Etruscan figures stretched out
on the lids of their sarcophagi, leaning
always on the left elbow, smiling with thick lips
heavily parted—dissolute features mutilated
and devoured by the ages—what comes to mind
are the *libri fatales* allotting these people
1,000 years. A prophecy so sharp and unequivocal
must actually have hurried Etrurian decadence.

Greeks and Etruscans disagreed on which substances
were appropriate for sculpture. Hard exact marble
was what the Greeks chose to personify their deities,
while the Etruscans used a soft porous volcanic rock
which soon crumbled, betokening imperfection.

Although Jaina and Hindu sculptures both used stone
their concepts of life could hardly be more different.
Writhing Hindu figures offer their voluptuous bodies
to every passion; whereas the nudity of Jaina statues,
like that of an ascetic, connotes absolute renunciation
of everyday mortal pleasures.

In early Buddhist art The Enlightened One
is never depicted anthropomorphically;
his presence is evoked by symbols.
At times the imprint of a foot sufficed.

Primitive artists emphasize what interests them most,
disdaining what they regard as superfluous.

Among the South African Imvani bushmen each picture
an artist paints is respected throughout his lifetime
and after his death for as long as a member of the tribe
can recall his name, who he was, or anything about him.
Until that time the rock surfaces he has embellished
with his vision are considered inviolate. I might add
that the last Bushman killed by the Boers was an artist;
he had been wearing a leather belt with 12 little horns,
each horn containing a carefully prepared pigment.

High on the wall of a cave in the Dordogne
archaeologists found a prehistoric bison
represented with remarkable individuality.
A cartoon of this bison on a piece of slate,
unmistakably by the same artist, was unearthed
in the *départément* of Ain. Now what this means
is that some man or woman or child of the Ice Age
admired the preliminary sketch so intensely
that he either bought the slate or stole it
and carried it all the way to Ain,
a distance of 188 miles.

A series of ancient wall paintings at Tel-el-Amarna
attracted archaeologists from around the world
until one night the farmer who owned the property
hacked the frescoes to pieces because the visitors
had been trampling his crops. Man measures everything,
of course, from its beginning to its end.

In the Pomeranian peat bog of Koppenow near Lauenburg
excavators turned up a substantial wooden box 26" long
with hollowed compartments holding a selection

of sword blades, axe heads, buttons, pins, rings
and ornamental pendants from the Bronze Age.
Evidently it belonged to a traveling salesman.

A bronze sword of Norwegian design
stamped with the seal of Pharoah Setekhy II
implies that Viking traders reached Egypt.
Tell me, how many voices have you heard
as eloquent as the past's mute artifacts?

Twenty meters below the roof of Djoser's step pyramid
in a granite burial chamber a German archaeologist
came upon the so-called earthly remains of its builder
—a leg bone. To be pyramidally extant, says Sir Thomas,
is a fallacy in duration.

Beneath the Gizeh pyramids are subterranean passages
carved from living rock which lead to the Sphinx
and its chapel. These corridors, stuffed with documents
of incredible significance, have never been excavated.

Napoleon, after climbing to the top of Cheops' pyramid,
announced that by his calculations it held stone enough
to build a wall around France. However, the dimensions
of a projected wall tell us less than imperial proclivities.

I've heard that when we look at the Great Pyramid
what we see is a symbol of an alien subconscious.
Perhaps. But Flinders Petrie's measurements
are more revealing, if you like facts. For example,
the orientation of the structure is so accurate
that it can be used to check compass errors.
Anyway, I remember my one visit to the place;
even now I can smell the unguents in the vault.
I won't go again. Next summer I'll try Paris
or Ibiza. Crete, maybe. If you haven't made plans
come along. We'll manage to amuse ourselves.

Excuse me, at times I forget where we are. Ah!
Not much is left of the great Alexandrian *pharos*

because of an earthquake in the 14th century
which sent its remnants tumbling into the harbor.
But if you know how to look beneath the surface
as clearly as a child you should see many things
apart from the ruins—all marvelous and unexpected.

Sometime during the 3rd century before Christ
an earthquake toppled the Colossus of Rhodes.
It lay undisturbed until the island was conquered
by Arabs, who sold the fallen statue to a merchant
with visions of profit in such a gleaming litter.
The chest of the Colossus measured 60' around,
and not many men could pick up one of its thumbs.
900 camels were needed to haul the bronze away.
That's about all we have—these few measurements
and a legend. Little outlives terrestrial elements
or indigent dreams of wealth.

Money, as might be expected, originated in Babylon
—a thin gold ribbon unwinding from a spool.

The dollar first saw daylight in Joachimstal.
A coin minted in this Bohemian village
came to be called a Joachimstaler. Hence thaler,
taler, etc. So much for the dollar.

Tell me, which would you prefer: a sharp bronze knife
or a peck of gold? Before answering, my friend,
it might be wise to reflect that values change.

Atahualpa's ransom, collected by Pizarro at Cajamarca
and paid not with coins but with cunningly fashioned
gold and silver objects, has been calculated at $19,851,642
in terms of contemporary purchasing power. All of these
several thousand precious objects were shipped to Spain
where, according to the royal decree of February 13, 1535,
they were distributed among the mints of Segovia, Toledo
and Sevilla to be melted. As far as we know, not one item
of Inca craftsmanship escaped Spain's omnivorous furnaces.
Was this intolerably materialistic? Or was it necessary?
Take into account the economy of 16th century Europe.

Among the treasures picked up by conquistadores
were ten planks of almost pure silver 3" thick,
10" wide and 20' in length! Not that I'm greedy,
you understand. I never forget certain truths.
I recognize that bread quiets the body's hunger
whereas flowers assuage the hunger of the soul
—which explains why the Moslem Emirs of Cordova
gave two loaves of bread for a single narcissus.

I'm careful also to remember the glassmaker's thanks
when he presented Tiberius with an astonishing cup
he had devised, which couldn't be shattered. If dropped
or hurled to the ground the glass would simply bend.
Tiberius had the glassmaker's head struck off at once,
sagaciously pointing out that if glass were pliant
men would begin to consider it as valuable as gold.
So you see I'm stuffed with a variety of thoughts;
earning my fortune's only one.

For various reasons, I suspect, our lives resemble those
of antiquity, but chiefly because we're just as gullible.
Traveling friars reported a fabulous country called Muc
beyond Cathaya in which there was a village with silver
walls and gold bulwarks; they spoke of 4,400 islands
in India whose lords were 64 crowned kings, and other
absurdities. You might be amazed at how many people
believe such rubbish, or that monsters abound in Korea.

There's a story that the King of Poland, Popelius,
together with his wife and children were eaten by rats
in the year 830. Do you think it's true?

Do you think Paracelsus was a eunuch?
He himself declared it better to be a castrate
than an adulterer, and women never accompanied him.
Furthermore, no authentic portrait shows him with a beard.
On the other hand, late in life he grew bald
which isn't a characteristic of eunuchs.
From Hirschvogel's etching we know
only that he was rachitic.
Well, you might ask

so what?
I'd be hard put to answer.
Maybe you'd best go your way and I'll
do whatever I feel like doing.
Chacun à son goût.

Ah-hemm! Do beards contribute to a man's
threatening appearance?

Did Zisca want a drum made out of his own skin?
Would such a drum put one's enemies to flight?

Do we escape from life on a ladder of cobwebs?

What lies beyond Cape Bojador? If you think you know
how can you be positive? Listen. In southern latitudes
do ships stick fast in a congealed gelatinous sea?
Does the sun burn sailors blacker than Negroes?
Do hideous creatures drag vessels into the depths?
The point is, you must appreciate the muddled nature
of our estate, and how all seems strange.

My daughter believes God organized the earth
with its waters, forests, mountains, cities, records,
events and memories in our minds a few seconds ago.
I explained that thousands of millennia are required
to establish a mountain range, and Palomar astronomers
have photographed nebulae 15,000,000 light years distant.
The more specifics I offered, the less she wanted to hear.
Your concept of a *deus ex machina* is quite preposterous,
I said. And I was right, although logically her argument
is impregnable. Paradox follows paradox.

Now I want to tell you something important.
Forget everything else, if you like,
but don't forget this. As the historian
Simon Dubrow was marked for death by the Nazis
he exhorted his companions to open their eyes
and ears. He urged them to memorize each detail,
each name, every sigh and the color of clouds

as well as the executioner's gesture. Circumscribed
as I might be, I've accepted this obligation.

Chelmno: 600,000.

Le 20 Août
Le Gardien de la Paix
Sitterlin René
est tombé ici pour . . .

Take a moment to study Goya's graphic lesson
The Third of May. Notice the implacable unanimity
of the soldiers in contrast to the individuality
of the victims. It's worth remembering.

Here's something else. A little while ago my grandson
stopped by for a visit. He didn't want to, of course;
his mother had insisted. I know how it is. He's eight,
and I rather suspect his friends were waiting outside.
He seemed quite proud of his polished paratrooper boots
and cadet uniform with a scarf, a beret and a green tunic
decorated with imitation battle stars and campaign ribbons.
Well, I'm not quite sure this is clear. Let me try again.

Look. There are now so many dead soldiers in Arlington
that a widow can no longer be buried beside her husband;
instead, his grave is deepened.

Look. The Pentagon is distributing armaments
under a program labeled "Food For Peace."

Among the Vietnamese there's a noticeable up-trend
in stillbirth, birth deformities and a condition called
hydatiform mole, which is a tumor of the placental
cord during pregnancy resulting from the widespread
spraying of crops with a compound of 2,4-D and 2,4,5-T,
the herbicidal defoliant "Agent Orange."

According to testimony presented at a meeting
of the American Academy for the Advancement of Science

the U.S. herbicidal program is eminently successful.
Of Vietnam's forests and arable land, twelve percent
has been either destroyed or convincingly damaged.
In some areas this is temporary; in other areas
it appears to be semipermanent. In the Mekong delta
a great many mangrove stands have been devastated,
causing erosion of stream banks and the destruction
of fisheries. Where there was once a proliferation
of tropical birdlife, now there are only buzzards.

Nothing exists, in Pliny's tremendous words,
more pitiable or presumptuous than Man.
Romans, for example, attempted to draw a line
between citizens they considered entitled
to the benefits of Empire and the belligerent
barbarians of the trans-Danubian wilderness
against whom civilization should be protected.

Suppose I reiterate what Pliny said,
because one certainty among uncertainties
is that nothing is certain, and not only
as nations but as individuals do we exceed
ourselves: *Solum ut inter ista vel certum
sit nihil esse certi nec quicquam miserius
homine aut superbius.*

Goethe, at the age of six,
thought the stars would never forget him.

Marconi, aboard his yacht *Electra* in the Mediterranean,
thought he was intercepting messages from Mars.

Gruithuisen thought he saw traces of a city on the moon,
and described not only its principal thoroughfare
but several subsidiary streets.

Loti saw a triumphal avenue on Easter Island
leading to submerged palaces,
which turned out to be a flow of lava.

Now, if you think those ideas were preposterous
listen to this: Diderot was convinced the blind
could be taught to read by their sense of touch!

Here's another. Swedenborg, after spending 31 years
in the Department of Mines, believed he stood under orders
from Jesus Christ to clarify the Bible.

Saint John of the Cross, feeling morally obligated,
licked out the sores of lepers.

Saint Margaret Marie Alocoque cleaned up the vomit
of a diseased patient with her tongue.

Allahu akbar! as the Arabs say. Certainly God is great.
However, it's worth remembering that religious mystics
tend to experience auditory and/or visual hallucinations,
such as the Apostle Paul who professed to hear a Voice
—a voice which we know succinctly expressed his own
repressed interrogation. Another example could be Christ,
although in view of the New Testament's unreliability
one must be cautious.

"Incomprehensible words tumbling uncontrollably
from the lips occurs most often among those of moderate
intelligence subjected to mystical or religious excitement,
when ordinary human emotions and sentiments
conflict with the demands of behavior or of conscience.
This phenomenon of glossolalia or xenoglossia is,
therefore, typical of persons accepting prevalent mores
with neither hesitation nor doubt." So says my uncle,
the Psychiatrist. I have a different interpretation.
I think these frantic people resemble minor poets
whose vision surpasses their ability to articulate it
—whose grotesque, pitiful and awkward mouthings
represent an effort to communicate to the rest of us
the very least of their terrifying intimations.

I must say that the muddled nattering of mystics,
aesthetes, scholars and their confused relatives

interests me less than a parliament of meadowlarks.
I consider strict control essential. My thoughts
display their own order, inevitable and coherent,
the least deviation from which is quickly apparent.
I confess to only one indulgence, and understandably
that couldn't be disclosed.

I admit to entering a crack in the universe
where worlds overlap, opening and shutting
like a door in the wind. Thus liberated
I observe a variety of scenes and places,
and speak with men, women and children
who presumably had vanished. One or two
or three might touch the imagination. So
by your grace:

Fata Morgana is a metropolis of the past—a harbor city
with alabaster walls, countless citizens and a palace.
It appears from time to time in the Straits of Messina.
Ever since the 16th century men have been speaking of it.
Although I, myself, have yet to see such an apparition
each day ends differently.

Now and then a nebulous Oriental city materializes
not far from Muir Glacier in Alaska. Streets, trees
and houses become visible, and curious buildings
surmounted by spires which are felt to be mosques.
Northwest Indians have known about it for generations
and two prospectors who were at work beside the glacier
reputedly saw its reflection in a pan of quicksilver.

In 734 A.D. when Moorish cavalry entered Oporto
seven Portuguese bishops, anticipating persecution
at the end of Christianity, set sail for the Azores,
relying on the sun to act as their compass.
Nothing was heard of them until the 15th century
when a Portuguese freighter bound for Lisbon
under the command of Captain Antonio Leone
was disabled by a storm and driven far to the west.
Finally a crescent-shaped island was sighted

and here, by the captain's log, they dropped anchor.
Going ashore, he and his men encountered Portuguese
who welcomed them gladly and inquired of them
if the Moors still troubled Spain. Captain Leone
reports that seven communities had been set up,
each with its bishop, and each had a cathedral
built of rock mortared with burnt seashell lime;
and when the crew attended mass they saw crucifixes
of gold, gold candlesticks and gold embroidered
altar cloth. The name of this island is Mayda
or Mam, or Asmaida. I'll tell you where it is.
In the vicinity of Lat. 46.23 N., Long. 37.20 W.
look twenty fathoms beneath the surface.

If we can observe other times and worlds
why not recapture noises from the past?
Scientists think it might be possible.
Suppose we actually hear the voice of Christ,
or that of Buddha or Mohammed. Say it's so,
what difference would it make? Embittered
by a cataract of public and private deception
surely most of us would continue unaffected.

Let me tell you about a woman who was deceived,
and what she did. Leif Ericcson set sail for Norway
from Greenland in the year 999, but a storm came up
and drove him far to the south among the Hebrides
where he met Thorgunna and made the usual promises
so that he could live with her. But autumn came
and Leif decided it was a good time to travel.
He gave Thorgunna a gold ring, a Greenland mantle,
a handsome belt of walrus tusk, and told her goodby.
Then she let him know that she would have his child
and she predicted ill fortune if he abandoned her,
saying "I foresee as much profit from this infant
as is due from our parting." Despite her prediction
Leif went away, and their child was feeble-minded.

Early in the 19th century in Fall River, Massachusetts,
the skeleton of a man adorned with metal ornaments

was dug up at the corner of Fifth and Hartley streets.
I have reason to think the bones were those of Thorvald,
Ericcson's son by another woman. Academicians argue,
insisting that in all probability the bones were those
of a protohistoric Wampanoag Indian. Now, because a fire
swept Fall River some years after the discovery, destroying
the museum where the skeleton was housed, neither my case
nor that of my opponents can be established. I'm uncertain
how I feel about this; but it just might be for the best
because mysteries attract us more than intelligible facts.

Drilling apparatus for an artesian well
on the Columbia plateau near the Snake River
threw up a baked clay figure from a depth of 320'
through a thick layer of solid basalt.
To date there's no explanation.

Natives of the Siwalik Hills discovered a tortoise
carapace 20' in length. How such a monstrosity
was able to move across this irregular terrain
nobody seems to know.

What kind of a beast was *Elephas ganesa*
with tusks 3' in circumference?

A mammoth's carcass excavated in Beresovka
was so well preserved that even the eyeballs
were intact. Unswallowed grass between its teeth
and inside its chest a great mass of clotted blood
testified to a violent death. Just what happened
we can't be sure, but all creatures come to an end
in their season. *Mutato nomine de te fabula narrat...*

My wife, echoing Novalis, complains that I hypnotize myself,
taking my own phantasmagoria for autonomous appearances.
Who knows, my friend? Who knows? I'm able to vanish
in a plume of smoke, tell time by a star, mint
ancient coins from fresh pennies and perform
many another marvel. Do you care if I don't bathe?

On one of the innumerable palm-leaf manuscripts
of the *Bhrigusamhita* at Hoshiarpur
I came across a description of my life,
as does every man who goes to consult it.
I'd been told the experience would inspire me
but I felt humiliated, and I haven't forgotten.
Of course, I don't forget much. Like the Jew
Dubnow, I memorize and memorize and memorize.

I remember lepers crawling through Hyderabad
as well as the voice of Lyndon Johnson.

Do you recall Johnson's apologia for murder?
I do, just as I recall the words of Job:
His remembrance shall perish from the earth
and he shall have no name in the street;
he shall be driven from light into darkness,
and chased out of the world.

Oh, you'd be pleased, Dubnow, in your German grave
by how acutely I remember. I've drawn portraits
in lake slime of the assistants: Rostow and Rusk.
Animals come late at night to appraise what I've done
and to urinate. Do you hear, Dubnow?

I've memorized the name of the United States ambassador
to Laos: G. McMurtrie Godley, who observes that although
we regret the terrible suffering of the Laotian people
it's better for them to die in their country's desolation
than for us to permit the advance of atheistic Communism.
I think, therefore, that Sir Thomas Browne must be correct:
the glory of one State depends on the ruin of another.

As usual, President Nixon is instructive:
We seek to do the work of righteousness.
Our power has always been used for
building the peace, never for breaking it;
for defending freedom and never for destr . . .

The two medical defects most often noted
in rural areas exposed to chemical defoliation
are cleft palate and *spina bifida*, a deformity
occurring when bone forms incompletely
around the tissue of an infant's spinal cord.

Ora pro nobis.

Night comes. Analysis of a day
concludes; what's important
turns around.

I'll play on my flute, softly
for a little while.

Constellations begin to take their places
like members of an orchestra,
one at a time—a comforting thought.

Comets, reputedly, are the souls of great men ascending.
This probably is so, because the night Vespasian died
a comet hurtled into view and the tomb of Augustus
was heard inexorably grinding open by itself.

When the fiery comet of 1664 was brought to his notice
Alphonsus VI of Portugal rushed toward the phenomenon,
stinging it with abuse and threatening it with a pistol.
As the Spaniards say: *Aunque la mona se vista de seda,
mona se queda.* Monkeys dressed in silk, etc.

Galileo, having recognized the phases of Venus
and anxious to claim credit without revealing
what he had learned until he could verify it,
published the anagram: *Haec immatura a me jam
frustra leguntur, o. y.* I've gathered this too soon.
Or, these letters could be rearranged to read:
Cynthiae figuras aemulatur mater amorum.
The mother of Love follows the phases of Diana.

Like Venus, the moon undergoes phases
which explains why it's come to symbolize

whatever is incomplete. That is, Woman.
The moon might be described as a harlot
reduced to this state by her dealings with men:
occasionally she rests, but always licentiously
returns to her tumultuous round. Such comparisons,
however, I find odious; I occupy myself with matters
of somewhat greater significance.

Spitzer and Baade have detected two star clusters
colliding beyond *Cygnus*, notifying the universe
of a stupendous meeting through reverberations
of inconceivable magnitude. Radio telescopes
are able to pick up signals that have traveled
several million years at the velocity of light;
yet the size of these galaxies suggests to astronomers
that the cataclysm might still be continuing.
If so, signals that are just now being emitted
will arrive long after the sun has folded upon itself
and only a thin cloud commemorates the earth's orbit.

Andromeda's stars aren't important, but opposite Mirach
is the Great Nebula, probably larger than the Milky Way,
visible as a hazy speck so faint that in order to see it
we must look a little aside.

A camera plate exposed to the area of Spica for 8 hours
reveals one dot of light thought to be a spiral galaxy
comprising billions of suns.

My friend the Astronomer points out Beta Lyrae
—a superb example of an eclipsing binary
which can be seen rising to its magnitude of 3.4
and falling to 4.1 during a period of 12 days,
21 hours and 45 minutes. Its component masses
are 21 and 10 times the diameter of the sun,
although the distance between them is just ⅓
the distance of the sun from the earth. Well,
what it means is that these rather large objects
are practically touching. Facts such as this
tend to excite me, but October's not far off
and I'm troubled by the restive leaves.

Somebody mentions that the earth spins each year
in its orbit 585 million miles around the sun
at a speed approximately 8 times that of a bullet.
If this motion stopped we would be consumed by fire,
in the judgment of certain authorities. Others doubt it.
All right, I say, but the argument seems irrelevant
so long as we live among men. I propose instead
that we cherish humanity—not that I expect
a particularly enthusiastic response.

Dum inter homines sumus, colamus humanitatem.
Seeds of knowledge have been granted us,
although not knowledge itself.

A boy wandering along the course of the ancient river
Pactolus picked up a potsherd that led archaeologists
to the ruins of Sardis. *Mirabile dictu!*

Venetian fishermen occasionally find entangled
in their nets a bronze hand or a chiseled marble
cornice dredged from the slime covering Metamauco,
which governed the Adriatic during the Dark Ages.
Ah well! a voice murmurs, what's the difference?
I submit that to stay ignorant of basilicas, mosques,
palaces, occurrences, common people and their Kings
who played out their time centuries before your birth
means that you remain a child. Of what value is life
if it's not woven on history's loom into other lives?

A millennium ago people around the Mediterranean
discussed Haithabu, a city larger than Cologne.
Honey, furs, wax, wine from the Moselle, amber
and Chinese silk, Friesian textiles, cattle, slaves,
horses, Mohammedan coins, swords, feathers, helmets
and almost everything else were traded here.
So much is forgotten so quickly.

Where are the walls of Epidauros?
*Nescire autem quid ante quam natus
sis acciderit, id est . . .*

On quiet windless days the columns and temples
of Baiae emerge from the Tyrrhenian's muddy floor;
fish wind down its streets past huge red lobsters
mindlessly ensconced in marble luxury.

 A Swiss Army officer rowing across Lake Neuchâtel
noticed among some tree stumps on the bottom
the blackened remnants of several bronze swords
in water so shallow that he touched them with an oar.
They belonged to a culture known as La Tène
whose origins antedate the imagination of Europe.
How could they have been overlooked for 20 centuries
this close to the surface of other men's lives?

Five hundred years ago the Roman Cardinal Colonna
ordered a team of divers brought from Genoa
to investigate a rumor of ancient ships
at the bottom of Lake Nemi in the Alban Hills.
Two hulks were encountered 10 fathoms down,
one measuring just under 100', the other 240'.
Hooks and ropes were employed to raise them
but the timbers collapsed; nothing was salvaged
except a broken statue. During the next century
they were explored by a diver named Demarchi,
but still the technical devices were inadequate.
They were seen again in the 19th century,
this time through the glass of a diving bell;
but not until Mussolini had the lake drained
could the ships be examined. Then it was learned
that they had belonged to the tyrant Caligula.
The planks of both hulls were artfully mortised,
overlaid by wool fibers impregnated with tar
and topped with lead sheets for protection
against algae, barnacles and worms. The oak decks
were decorated with mosaics, the staterooms
furnished with mirrors and terra cotta lamps,
and provision had been made for hot baths.
By Mussolini's order a museum was built
and people arrived from almost everywhere
to marvel at them. But World War II erupted

and what Nature had preserved for 2,000 years
was promptly obliterated by Allied bombers.
As the Italians say: *Ogni medaglia ha il suo
rovescio.*

The ships of an earlier emperor vanished more inexplicably
if somewhat less explosively than Caligula's pleasure boats:
Alexander's entire fleet disappeared from the Persian Gulf.
History is silent as to whether a storm scattered the ships
or whether the admiral, overwhelmed by a grandiose dream,
sailed into a sunset of rumors. There's been speculation
that certain American Indian tribes could be the descendants
of these lost Macedonians—probably because it pleases us
to imagine fanciful things.

My uncle claims to have traced the course of Yucatán Indians
back to those Israeli tribes expelled from Assyria by Sargon
in 721 B.C. There are sculptural representations of elephants,
he insists, on the façade of a Mayan temple at Palenque.
Frankly, I don't see much connection between Assyrians
and "elephants," but obviously he does. When I asked him if
these beasts might not be tapirs, which have a long snout,
he replied with considerable annoyance that the animals
also have tusks, which tapirs haven't. So there we are.

Botanists searching for the origin of Indian corn
eventually discovered on the Guatemalan plateau
a grassy plant called *teocentli* which resembles corn,
although lacking the characteristic cob and stalk.
Because these plants are capable of interpollination
a relationship was established on the assumption
that *teocentli* had been found and subsequently
cultivated by ancestors of the Maya. Somewhat later
it was learned that to produce corn from *teocentli*
would require 20,000 years—granting these people
not only high intelligence and agricultural experience
but a deliberate procedure for modification.
In other words, a familiar lesson was repeated.

Mayan chronology opens at 4 *ahau*, 8 *cumhu*:
3,400 years prior to the commencement

of their earliest monument. What this means
is that an event of staggering significance
has been dated for posterity's benefit.
What it was is anybody's guess.

So much for the past. Minutes are more precious
than centuries. The earth has existed as it does now
for 1,832,000,000 years.

Mathematicians predict that sooner or later
more nations will be spread across the universe
than the total number of people who have ever lived.
I answer that I'll believe it when I see it.

I'm told that because of the sun's orbit
we circle the gravitational center of our galaxy
once every 200 million years. My congratulations
to whoever figured this out. Just the same,
I'd rather listen to Boccherini.

I've heard about the Beams Ultracentrifuge
which revolves 1½ million times per second.
I apologize for not being terribly impressed.
The fact is, I'm much more amazed by feathers,
equestrians, Kwakiutl necklaces, the pendulous
bosom of my beloved wife Margaret, or that
odd awkward hippopotamus our daughter modeled
and tried so hard to bake in the kitchen stove.
What I'm suggesting is that our satisfactions
are primarily sensual. *Il n'y a rien de mieux
à faire que de s'amuser.*

If you don't understand why I speak figuratively
remember: this is a song for a single voice. That is,
a monody. Listen.

Between the elm and the vine sympathy exists,
but antipathy is known between the vine
and the bay. The vine does not love the bay,
nor his smell, and kills him if he grows near.
Similarly, the burr can't endure the lintle,

although the olive and the myrtle embrace
not only in their branches but in their roots.
The implications of such mysteries is obvious.

The leaf of the fig has especial significance
because of its resemblance to the womb,
and with its stem the sistrum of Isis.

I've told you before I never learnt to give love
like most men. I love immortal things.
I visit Anna Codde in the Netherlands; in Castile
my stout Moorish Queen. Others beg my attention
here or there. I'm fond of a fastidious lady
with thin hands clasped above a red sash.
Rogier Van der Weyden loved her, I suspect.
Oh, I could name several. But ultimately
what's the use? *Cui bono?* so to speak.
Nobody cares about another's passion.

I think the impression you have of me is false.
You should understand that because I abhor craftiness
and duplicity I can't recognize those traits in others.
I despise cowardice and remain indestructibly loyal
to such friends as I select. Concerning money
I don't have much respect for it. I know, of course,
that these characteristics are worse than useless
and I should sensibly resign myself to disappointment,
if not to failure. There's no use telling me.
I agree. However, I regard logical eventualities
just as I look upon weeds growing beside the path.
In other words, the winding descent is pleasant;
I help myself to joy and beauty wherever I find it.

I doubt if we cry only for the unhappy past,
nor for happy events we cherish;
but for childhood with its illusions,
and the inevitable separation from what we love.

Pas la couleur, mon ami; rien que la ...

I? Who am I?
A fugitive singer.
Songs I make,
butterflies of song
that bloom in the soul
for the heart's delight.

I've grown fat, I admit,
although my hair's still black
and neatly combed.
I affect smoked glasses
and enjoy a cigar in the evening.
My wife seems rather distant
but that doesn't displease me.
Comfortably, side by side
we sleep away the years,
seldom touching. Now
can't you guess my name?

I'm not Goya, although I resemble him
as he decorated the walls of his house
near Manzanares with bizarre paintings
expressing his bitter concept of a world
that brings disillusionment and sadness.

Look. People stare at me
although I honor none of them
by recognition. Not one.
Well, what do you say?

Look, I've just written my name in the dust
beside the door, because calligraphy is important.
I doubt if it will be disturbed for 300 years.
What I wish to explain is that fitness of form
survives, despite the attrition of time.

Let me point out to you that a wise man's mind
is similar to the state of the world beyond the moon,
perpetually serene.

Here's some good advice:
mistrust those whose opinions change
more than once.
Verbum sapienti sat est.

Sooner or later you'll be told that Heaven and Earth
are very much alike. Don't believe it. Celestial bodies
are carried about in their orbs without impediment
or interruption to continue truly on their courses
for innumerable ages and to make their conversations,
as Burton puts the business, while common men are urged
by numerous difficulties and diverse oppositions,
hindrances crossing their endeavors and desires.
If this bewilders you, never mind. Listen.

Ladislaus, King of Bohemia at the age of eighteen,
rich, surrounded by friends, ready to be married,
sickened and died in less than a day and a half.
So it is with kings as with kingdoms, provinces and
townships; they have their period and are consumed.
Babylon, the greatest city anybody ever visited,
is nothing except dusty walls and mounds of rubbish.
Names are left, not much else.

Now I'll tell you about the pygmy King of Poland,
Uladslaus Cubitalis, whose victories surpassed those
of any of his predecessors. I doubt if you know why;
but the most puissant and sagacious men are smallest
because their souls necessarily have contracted.
There's more truth in this than you suspect.

A Milanese prince, told that one of his subjects
hadn't stepped outside the gate in half a century,
issued an edict commanding him never to leave;
at which the citizen became so anxious to escape
that presently he fell sick and died of grief.
Laugh if you like. Myself, I wouldn't.

Here's something for your amusement. My mother writes:
I have seen demons cast out of people, the sick healed,

people speaking in tongues—just as the Bible promised.
By God's truth you and I are able to change the world.
Every night on my knees I pray for someone to reach you
because your Heavenly situation depends on it...
Her letter reminds me of Vrencken's to Burgravius
in which mention is made of an optical instrument
that will enable us to see past the horizon!
If I choose to believe one, why not the other?
I'll believe both when I know the complement of men
that can stand together on the surface of the earth.
Reputedly this figure is 148,456,800,000,000
but I'm skeptical of neat answers.

The Unicorn, they say, is nothing except an oryx
whose two horns have unnaturally grown together.
Perhaps. All one should state with conviction
is that our wishes and our beliefs embrace
as surely as the myrtle and the olive intermingle.

We used to think fossilized elephant bones
might be the bones of legendary heroes;
and the sea, where it stands above the earth,
would overflow except for God's intervention.

It was thought that in Lucomoria,
which is a province of Russia,
men lie asleep from the 27th of November,
benumbed with cold like swallows or frogs
until the 24th of April when they awake,
rise and go complacently about their business.

It was believed that the Danube corresponded
to the Nile, because Herodotus so drew them
on his map of the world. But now we understand:
he did this out of a great passion for symmetry.

Apples were thought to be the food of the dead,
which explains their presence in primitive graves.
Nuts were considered a symbol of fertility.

Prehistoric circles of stones were regarded as relics
of lost civilizations, or perhaps the petrified bodies
of men and women who danced on a holy day.
Delusions and illusions accompany us.

I once knew a man who thought he was Atlas
supporting Heaven on his shoulders,
another who thought we was a leather bag
stuffed with wind. And in Ferrara
there was a baker who often felt his limbs,
convinced that they were made of butter,
and at last was unable to walk past a fire
or even sit outside in the sun.

How do we separate fiction from reality?
Medical students recited Galen
to the effect that some particular bone
belonged to the breast at the very moment
it was being extracted from the foot.

How do we decide what to believe? Or whom?
Napoleon contemplated building a canal
from the Red Sea to the Mediterranean
but abandoned the idea after being warned
by his engineers that the Indian Ocean
would inundate Egypt to a depth of 4'.

The Marquis de Laplace mathematically demonstrated
that no difference could exist between the levels
of the Red Sea and the Mediterranean. Nevertheless
his demonstration was rejected. Why? Well, because
popular tradition argued against it.

Here's something fascinating: Pharaoh Necho II
ordered a canal cut from the Red Sea to Bubastis
on the Nile delta. Although 120,000 lives were lost
he continued the work until informed by an oracle
that he was assisting the Persians. A century later
his canal was completed by Darius.

Fifteen hundred years before Christ's birth two stone obelisks
measuring 100' in length and each weighing 700 tons
were brought up the Nile from the temple of Hatshepsut
at Karnak. From the dimensions of these tremendous pillars
we can estimate the size of the vessel that carried them,
but how such a ship could be constructed entirely of wood
without breaking beneath its own weight, we have no idea.
What I'm trying to explain is that the past and present
and future all are stuffed with marvels—events, sights,
odors and sounds eluding the feeble grasp of our senses.

Imagine, if you will, Sir Isaac Newton,
riddled with genius, confronted by a radio
whose significance he would never doubt
but whose purpose he could not appreciate.

We know that as we approach the speed of light
time contracts: the year becomes the month.
And if a man on the surface of a dwarf star
fell ⅓" he would disintegrate in a split second.
These are facts. About other matters, we quarrel.
Esquimaux, for instance, claim that the Milky Way
is the track of a raven walking across snow;
Sumerians believe it to be a flock of sheep;
Chinese argue that it must be a celestial river
rushing toward the Taho—that preeminent stream
where the mother of the sun washes her children
before she lets them play in the sky. Obviously
opinions vary.

It has been established that within 10 miles of us
lie all the natural materials we could ever use.
Do you doubt it? Listen: one cubic mile of sea water
holds 150 million tons of solid material, including
almost every element. And the nature of common granite
would astound you. Ordinary igneous rock contains
aluminum, titanium, lead, iron, copper, vanadium,
nickel, manganese, chromium and tungsten in quantities
sufficient to humble billionaires.

Oh, I could go on discussing everyday rocks
but I prefer to talk about emeralds. Now look,
if you have an emerald here's how its vigor
should be tested. First, with the jewel in your hand
draw a circle around a toad. Next, place the emerald
squarely in front of the toad's eyes. Before long
one of two things will happen. If the jewel is weak
the power of the toad's gaze will cause it to explode,
but if the gem prevails the toad himself will burst.
On my reputation I swear this is so. I've seen it.
After a very short lapse of time during which
the toad unswervingly kept its gaze on the gem
I saw the emerald crack like a nut and fly apart.
Then the toad, which hitherto had stood immovable,
withdrew as though freed of some baleful influence.
I affirm that this is the truth, that my every word
is true, and I am Albertus Mag...

Q-K2.
P-QN4.

Everybody wants to know what the game signifies.
Clarification exhausts me. I concern myself
with humanity at the point where judgments
coalesce. Furthermore, I dislike being
unexpectedly wakened. Among the Masai
a sleeper is never abruptly aroused
for fear his soul might be alarmed
and not return, and the sleeper will die.

Keep this in mind: not many freedoms are left;
those few we have exist in the realm of dreams.

Lat. 26.12 S.; Long. 118.10 W.
Past midnight. I don't know the date,
not that it matters. I can make music
and track Orion.

I suppose my father's disturbed about me
because in his view I act like a daughter,

but is it my fault if I'm different?
Because I enjoy walking in the meadow
and sometimes bake bread or read poetry
or entertain my friends with the flute
should I be penalized?

I think I've already suffered more than my share;
even as a child I wasn't young—though in exchange
I've been granted the plenary powers of ubiquity,
which means I travel at leisure across endless fields
and through vast palaces. *Il rit bien qui rit le* . . .

It was suggested that a green baize cloth
be placed across my eyes each afternoon
for two hours, just as one covers the cage
of a canary when one does not wish it to sing.
I, always obedient, complied. Do as you wish
I thought to myself. And my dreams multiplied
beneath the cloth. I guessed that I was myself
merely a dream translating a dream. Etc. Etc.

Coulton dreamt of a monstrous rolling sphere
which he described as a congeries of spheres
fitted like the layers of an onion,
each with its independent revolution,
that grew before him with frightful rapidity
until there seemed no limit to its size.
It was far too immaterial to roll over him;
the horror existed not in what it might do
but in the nature of the thing itself,
as well as in what it was doing to itself,
although neither in his dream nor afterward
could he explain why the sphere should not be
precisely what it was, or appeared to be,
nor why it ought not to have done as it did.
Freiheit ist nur in dem Reich der Träume.

Coventry Patmore dreamt six weeks after his wife's death
that she lay dying, and awoke with indescribable relief
only to remember the truth.

My sister told me she had dreamt of her belly
as a garden out of which swarmed a thick growth
of blood-saturated weeds. She asked what it meant.
It means war in Asia will continue and horrifying
mutations proliferate. Why? Because we're governed
by the arrogance of kings.

To determine whether the Gothic or Roman missal
would be more appropriate for religious services
Alfonso VI ordered both books thrown into a fire,
saying he would approve whichever survived.
When the Gothic missal refused to burn
Alfonso threw it to the flames again.
Now do you understand?

The stars, more fortunate than men,
are governed by ineluctable laws
and prayer has no power over them.
It's possible to predict their motions,
that's all—though I wish to point out,
as Nietzsche did, that agreement between us
is neither necessary nor desirable.

Sir James Jeans, whose opinion I respect,
suggests we view the universe as a thought
rather than focus on its mechanistic aspect.
I accept the proposal, conditionally;
I've not forgotten Hegel's demonstration
that there could be no more than 7 planets,
nor Pliny's remark about pitiable presumption.

Svante Arrhenius postulates that Venus
might be in an earlier period of evolution
than Earth—choked with steaming jungles,
populated by monstrosities. I have my doubts.

One thing I don't question is that space curves
and returns finally upon itself. Because of this
we look toward ourselves in every direction.

At Sippar near Babylon was an astronomical school
where in 7 B.C. the great conjunction of Jupiter
and Saturn was observed. Now, in those credulous days
Saturn was believed to hold unusual significance
for the western lands, and Jupiter of course
was, as it still is, the royal planet. All of which
means that their convergence must have been an event
whose ramifications should be explored. Consequently
I see nothing improbably about the hypothesis
of three venerable Jewish astronomers from Babylon
traveling west to find out if a miracle had occurred.
But fable or fact, it's unimportant. Present riddles,
present relevance.

My uncle, a physicist of some competence
if minor brilliance, constantly argues with me
about our limitations. Again and again
he reiterates the dead laws of Aristotelian
logic: triangles can't have 4 angles, etc.
I tell him he's living in learned ignorance;
only fools neglect fundamentals, he replies.
An ass-headed God keeps the Gate of Heaven,
I say; think whatever you like, he answers.
Well, thou art in the end what thou art.

Copernicus, persuaded that the universe must somehow
be harmonious, directed his studies with abrupt disregard
for Authority. Unlike those phlegmatic medieval students
passively reciting Galenic absurdities, here was a man
adding and multiplying the evidence. Too bad he's gone;
a little graduate study wouldn't hurt my uncle.

As a rule, the greater the intelligence
the higher the degree of cooperation.
Because this is so, Tycho Brahe's obstinate
refusal to record his observations puzzles us.
Legend says he considered writing a book
beneath his dignity. That could be the reason
but maybe there was another. Riddles evolve
and intertwine, and what light illuminates them

isn't apt to fall from the sky. I've told you
once: *Verbum sapienti sat est.*

Look. How we interpret life depends first of all
on the information collected by our eyes, which matured
according to the prevalent type of radiation—namely,
the sun's light. But if the sun weren't what it is
or if we had happened to develop someplace else,
perhaps subjected to the radiation of a red giant,
we would observe things which are at present invisible,
just as certain ideas governing the tide of humanity
rise and fall undetected by mediocre sensibilities.
Let's put it like this: in the field of electromagnetic
radiation some sixty octaves have been discovered,
yet only one takes the form of visible light. We are,
therefore, in the unreasonable position of somebody
struggling to listen to a symphony composed of notes
almost entirely outside his auditory range.

Maturation of thought is both promoted and limited
by language—not as immutably as solar radiation
determines sight, but more than might be expected.
Here's one instance: Christ is very similar to God
yet not identical. *Homoiousios*, not *homousios*.

Here's another: despite the research of early scholars
who believed *Rus* evolved from the Slavic *rusyi*
meaning blond, it derives from the Finnish *Ruotsi*,
referring to people from the land of Roslagen.

Here's the last: *German* comes from the Latin
germani which means brothers or brothers-in-arms,
a reference to the discipline and fanaticism
Roman soldiers met on that early frontier.
Not much changes. *Eisen und Blut.*

Ravensbrück: 92,000.

If it comforts you to forget,
do so by all means.

As for myself,
I never forget anything.

The Cradle is a German invention.
It's essentially a bathtub
studded on the inside with knobs
and spikes. The victim,
bound, is rocked like a baby.
If you can understand this
you understand Germany.

The Cauldron, as practiced in Holland and Belgium
by the Holy Inquistion, consists of a metal dish
or bowl just large enough to accommodate several mice,
which is strapped upside down on the heretic's stomach.
When burning coals are placed on the inverted surface
the mice attempt to escape by burrowing. So as you see
the penalty for heterodox thoughts can be serious.
Plus ça change, plus c'est la même. Yesterday's truth
persists.

Medieval Church authorities considered it advisable
to prevent condemned prisoners from saying anything
while being escorted through the streets to the stake.
However, they wanted this prohibition kept secret.
The problem was solved by pulling the prisoner's tongue
through an iron ring and searing the tip. After that
the prisoner could be led publicly to his execution
without a gag, and no matter how much he talked
nobody was quite able to understand what he said.
The citizens responded to these last blurred warnings
with stupefied amazement, which is worth remembering.

The Spider was a simple, effective device:
two short iron bars terminating in claws
which projected from a wall. It was designed
for women, who were dragged across the talons
until their breasts had been clawed away.
The inventors, of course, were priests.

In the practice called Squassation
a prisoner's hands were tied behind his back,
iron weights were attached to his feet,
and he was unceremoniously hoisted by the hands
until his head reached the level of the pulley
where he was permitted to dangle a while.
Suddenly he was dropped without warning
almost, but not quite, to the ground.

They say there's no conceivable limit to suffering.
One who has suffered until he thinks he knows all of it
can, in fact, be made to suffer more. They say its nature
is like a quantity of gas pumped into an empty room
which fills up the space completely and evenly,
regardless of size. Yet, if we are to believe Spinoza,
suffering subsides as soon as we create its picture:
*Affectus, qui passio est, desinit esse passio simulatque
eius claram . . .*

Aristotle and Demosthenes both spoke favorably
of torture. This suggests, contrary to popular belief,
that its appeal is not restricted to Philistines.

Nabis of Sparta ordered his victims put to death
with an instrument cunningly fashioned to resemble
his wife.

Achas, fifth son of Salamona, was pounded to death
in a brazen mortar.

Two sisters of Simeon, the Bishop of Salencia,
being accused of molesting the Empress by witchcraft,
were quartered and their bloody pieces tied to posts
around which the Empress was borne in a canopied litter.
So it goes. Yet not until the humiliating agony of Christ
was torture actually encouraged and given the impetus
with which we have become familiar. *Vae victis!*

Don't forget, today we live in a Quaker world
where God blesses us in the sign of our puissance.

You might find it instructive to visit the Pentagon.
If moral nuances happen to be your bag, as they are mine,
you should have no trouble reading the summons to violence,
degradation and malfortune. The air strangely grows fetid,
voices subside and a dark odor spreads. Luther's words
grope forth:

I am the turd that is ready and the world is the open anus.

A few weeks ago my brother got back from the war.
At night I hear him groaning and twisting about
as though trying to escape. Friends pity him
but I don't. Nor do I condemn him. Those responsible
must be judged by their victims.

At Fort McClellan, Alabama, is a chemical school
where soldiers from 36 nations are instructed
in the use of germs and poison gas—how each agent
ought to be distributed, which is most effective
under which conditions, etc. Well, Diodorus Siculus
writing in the 1st century mentions a mutilated
and scattered god. Can you make anything of this?

Look. Anthropologists studying the Aztec nation
have concluded that when the first Europeans arrived
it was already nourishing within itself the seeds
of anarchy—war and human sacrifice—and the people
would very soon have revolted against their rulers.
Spanish oppression simply substituted one debacle
for another. Do you follow me? No? All right, listen.

The faces of priest-like figures on altars and stelae
in the ruined cities of Yucatán were brutally violated.
What animated the Maya to attack their spiritual leaders
we can only guess, but remote echoes ring toward Rome.

Searching for causes of the Crusades
we find constant sermons on the Antichrist
and a Day of Judgment. Entire generations
ultimately grew hagridden by images

of forthcoming disaster. Historians argue
as to whether or not this grim urgency
has been scheduled afresh. If you know,
tell me.

Is our God militant and wrathful?
Does He fight beside us against His enemies?

The word *God* is spelled with four letters
in virtually every language except English.
Idga is the Tartarian word, *Addi* is Turkish,
Zenc is Wallachian, *Doga* is Croation, *Rogt*
is Dalmatian, *Eher* is Tyrrhenian, *Chur* is
Etrurian, *Oese* is Margarian, and so forth.

The implication of God in Anglo-Saxon is Goodness
whereas the word Man intimates Wickedness. For example,
after the Patriarch of Antioch had rebuked Reynald
de Châtillon for attempting to blackmail the Emperor
Reynald had him smeared with honey and chained to a roof
where insects drove him mad.

When Raymond of Antioch was beheaded
his silver-mounted skull was delivered to Baghdad.
Exeunt omnes.

The Bible was created in Asia, in the sand
of Arabia, in the desert of Judea,
in the court of the temple of the Jews,
in music schools of the prophets of Bethel
and Jericho, in Babylonian palaces,
on the banks of the Chebar
and in the heart of the West.
It contains not a single mistake,
according to my mother. One may look
unsuccessfully among its 50 authors, 66 books,
1,189 chapters and 31,173 verses
for the first error.
Fiat lux.

Biblical divination during the 5th century
became so common that several ecclesiastic councils
expressly forbade it as injurious to religion
and redolent of idolatry. But throughout history
every edict suppressing this practice has failed.
Oremus.

Just as the oldest divinatory technique
is haruspicy, the most acceptable religious offerings
always have been blood and virginity.
Mirab...

When the great temple of Tenochtitlán was dedicated
it's said that 20,000 hearts were provided.
United States records concerning the Orient,
however exemplary, prove somewhat less accurate.
Look, I'm trying to explain that what's important
is to rectify and recreate. Three centuries ago
Grunnius Corocotta Porcellus' testament was memorized
by every schoolboy, but how well could you recite it?
So much for popularity. What we commit to memory
should be worth the attention of our descendants
—such as the fact that after Nong Khai was bombed
by the United States Air Force a pregnant woman
who had been gravely injured was offered $20
by the American government. Do you understand?

I've read in *Cent vingt journées de Sodome*
that Nature causes all of us to be born equal,
and if Fate as been pleased to disturb this plan
it's our responsibility to correct the mistake.
That is, to repair the usurpations of the stronger.
When I showed this passage to my brother-in-law
he answered with phrases such as "moral commitment,"
"allies" and "obligation." During the tenure of
the insane and decadent Caligula, I pointed out,
dexterity with a beheading sword was regarded as highly
as military marksmanship today. Well, he pretended
I'd lost my wits, but both of us know better.

Who am I? Let's forget the question.
Say that I'm a fugitive
singer of flowers.
you know the rest.

Say that I believe with Origen
the dead return to earth as spheres.
Say anything you like.
Say that I can't find what I'm searching for,
but I'll never give up traveling.

I've read the account of Friar Johannes Carpini
who crossed the northeast quadrant of the world
six centuries ago; I've heard of Presbyter John,
as well as the land of Hudirat; of the Parossitae
who never eat, but inhale the odor of cooking flesh.
I have learned how Jeroslaus, the Duke of Soldal,
was poisoned by Tartars. His body turned blue.
I've studied the journal left by William de Rubruk
of the Minorite Order who visited the East,
who reminds us it is written in Ecclesiasticus
concerning the wise man that he shall travel
to foreign lands.

I own a letter by Hernando del Pulgar
dated the 2nd of February, 1492. Listen:
He pretends the earth is round
and that necessarily there must exist,
beyond the ocean, a world to act as counterpoise
to the world we inhabit; that, in all events
if there do not exist beyond the ocean
countries entirely distinct from our continent,
still he asserts that by sailing west
a vessel must sail completely around the world
until it reach the eastern shores of Asia,
and the gold-roofed city of Cipango
described by Marco Polo.

My uncle often says all things are possible
to him that believeth; yet is it not extravagant

if countries exist in a line beneath our feet,
where men walk downward as certainly as flies
cross a fretted roof? Would anyone dispute this?
I altogether agree with Cosmas Indicopleustes
that the world is square and like a chessboard
terminable. Flat it cannot help but be,
surrounded on every side by water, beyond which
lies the Abyss. Thus, on their maps and charts
Arab geographers always draw toward the extremity
a black and skinny hand, emblematic of the Devil's claw
reaching for mortals who are rash enough to explore
outside boundaries.

Currents flow; stories end.
The part of us that sees is untroubled,
Plotinus asserts.

Some say we live among tints more bewildering
than the colors of an autumn forest.
Crescite et multiplicamini et replete terram.

Permit me to tell you about Sor Juana Inés de Asbaje,
born to a Spanish father and a Creole mother
in the village of San Miguel Neplantla
close to Amecameca at the foot of Popocatepetl.
Nothing meant as much to her as knowledge
because early in life she guessed love's limits.
At the age of six she disguised herself as a boy
and tried to register at the university. Later
when she was allowed to begin studying grammar
she cut off a length of her hair as punishment
because she thought it unreasonable for a head
clothed in hair to be otherwise so naked.
Eventually, murmuring began against her incessant
inquiries and she was ordered to quit studying,
which she did—yet continued to examine and admire
everything on earth, saying that as no creature exists
in which the *re fecit Deus* is not manifest,
so none can fail to stun the understanding,
provided it is reflected upon as it should be.

Reflect upon the following,
which is simpler than you think:
Atta unsar thu in himinam.
Weihnai namo thein.
Quimai thiudinassus sijaima,
swaswe jah weis afletam thaim
skulam unsaraim.
Jah ni briggais uns in fraistubujai.
Ak lausei uns af thamma ubilin,
unte theina ist thiudangardi,
jah maths, jah wulthus in aiwins. Amen.
As you've guessed, it's a translation
of our familiar Christian prayer
by Ulphilas, Bishop to the Western Goths
for those less fortunate.

Remember, miracles of the soul
are great than those of Heaven.

Remember that St. Bernard of Clairvaux
experienced a doubling of time
because of his earthly love affair
with Eternity.

Philipp Mainländer held us to be fragments of a God
who long ago destroyed himself. Don't forget.

Joseph's garment, snout of a serafim, Saint Michael's sweat,
Our Lord's teeth, rays from the star over Bethlehem . . .

Ora pro nobis.

An experienced salesman of Indulgences,
one Tetzel, arriving in Saxony with a catalogue
of pardons for sins past, present or as yet
uncommitted, so infuriated Martin Luther
that he compiled his great list of grievances
resulting in the Protestant Reformation.
Expelled by one door, the Devil reenters
though another.

Satan, as is well known, assumes various shapes
in order to torment us; thus malice in animals, birds
and insects should be taken for granted.

At Valois a bull was strangled for goring a man.
At Falaise a sow that killed a child was publicly
mutilated. Tit for tat.

A host of beetles that ravaged the vineyard
of Saint Julius was commanded to appear
in King's Court. When they neglected the summons
a lawyer was appointed to speak on their behalf.
This case was argued for a number of years.
It sounds ludicrous, but old persuasions linger.
Mutato nomine de te fabula narratur.

Sixteen women accused of witchcraft
arrested by the prosecutor of Lorraine
promptly hanged themselves in their cells,
so redoubtable was his passion for justice.
Can you think of a parallel?

For having cast a spell over King Louis X
Enguerrand de Marigny was hanged at Montfaucon.
As you see, the citizens of every age
live subject to society, stuffed like geese
at Christmas from beak to pinfeathers
with preposterous beliefs and spurious values,
their minds netted by philosophical or mystical
illusions working to create false realities.

German soldiers during the Great War
carried bats' wings as protection against bullets;
theologians see in their hearts Communism,
last-born of Satan. God help us.

Dragons, some assert, are the cause of eclipses
because they swallow the luminaries; I doubt this,
although I believe the child prostitute attracts
the ambassador just as the first plover eggs
fetch high prices.

I believe, too, that the praying mantis
is a blasphemous grasshopper
caricaturing the pious.

I believe that the religious stigmata
of Saint Francis, fleshy excrescences
resembling the nails of the Crucifixion,
represent the first recorded instance
of a peculiar neurotic manifestation
imitated with avidity during later ages.
Dr. Imbert Gourbeyre lists 340 such cases,
a majority involving women.

My wife Judith, mouthing lost languages,
weeps, pulls her hair and grovels on the floor
while I genuflect before traditional sciences
that heartlessly analyze shocking phenomena:
Hysterical verbal automatism should be regarded
as a bridge between autonography and the ecstatic
mouthings of trance mediums; the process
of obscuration reveals a rhythmic character
coinciding with the br . . .

An alteration of personality by no means unusual
is exemplified in the conversion of Saul.
We are not surprised to hear of a subsequent
affliction that embarrassed him—probably a tic
or stammering. It's also highly probable that
unknown to himself he reverted at opportune moments
to fanaticism.

Five centuries ago in Franconia a neatherd,
one John Beheim, took it upon himself
to become a prophet. So successful was he
that women abandoned their distaffs,
tradesmen their shops, servants their masters
and children ran away from their parents.
At last the Bishop of Würtsburg decreed
that the presumptuous rustic be arrested
and burnt—which could have been predicted
as easily as Saul's uncontrollable mannerism.

Perhaps the mother of Devotion is indeed Ignorance
and life carries us hoodwinked like hawks. Who knows?
During King Stephen's reign the miracles of Christ
were imitated by Eudo de Stellis. And for good measure
he built a castle in the air. As my mentor has said:
Since our longest Sun sets at right descensions
and makes but winter arches, and therefore
it cannot be long before we lie down in darknesse
and have our light in ashes; Since the brother
of death daily haunts us with dying mementos,
and time that grows old itself . . .

Lat. 12.09 S.; Long. 84.16 W.
Years pass
like the arm of a weaver's shuttle.

Peruvian women, before starting a new fabric,
ask God's blessing.

On the Paracas peninsula in subterranean rooms
400 mummies were found flexed and wrapped
in superb shawls, elaborate robes and turbans
decorated with exquisite polychrome embroidery
—possibly the finest textiles ever loomed.
Nothing whatever is known about these people,
not their language, not even their tribal name,
nothing but the style and quality of their weaving
and that they used the desert for mummification.
Caylla llapi Pununq . . .

We have no idea what the Inca called themselves;
the word simply refers to the one that governed.
And knot-string records are completely useless
without the help of professional Rememberers,
the last of whom is long since dead, so *quipus*
are now nothing but curious lifeless strings.
They did not, like the Maya, carve hieroglyphs
or, like the Aztec, make folding books with rebus
writing. No Inca journal exists in any form,
and throughout their tremendous history

we can be positive of just one date: 1532.
That was the year Pizarro found them.

Pages of historical detritus turn like the leaves
of a mouldering manuscript:

Between the strata of two great civilizations in Tarsus
archaeologists came upon a bed of earth 5' thick
undisturbed by any trace of human activity.

There are places where 100 successive beds of coal
have formed. What this signifies
is that the sea flooded the land 100 times
but invariably retreated.

Debris from Scandinavia once filled the North Sea basin,
creating land from Norway to the Low Countries,
and the monumental ancestor of the Rhine
flowed across it with the Thames as a tributary.

In Geiseltal lignite we discover ferns
from every continent
torn to pieces, yet with the nervature intact.

Have you been listening,
or do you hope for quick profit?
The ruins of a prehistoric temple
built with 130 million bricks
lie unmolested in the Moche valley.
Market these bricks at . . .

Reindeer attracted to campgrounds and villages
by a desire for salt, which they lick from urine,
are easily captured. A modest capital inv . . .

Eggs laid by the roc, or *Aepyornis*,
measure 13" in length, 9" in width.
Each shell holds 2 gallons of fluid.
At current pr . . .

Then how, if we are rich,
is it possible to be poor?

Let me put the matter like this:
I'm a man, a woman, a boy,
a girl, a plant, a bird, a beast,
a fish. Now, would you agree
or regard such a statement
as demonstrably false?

Do you accept or reject fabulous doctrine?
Be careful how you answer, my friend;
you could be less sophisticated than you think.

If Nature urges the reindeer to lick urine
perhaps we, too, would find it beneficial.
Do you suppose a cup taken every morning
for a few days would alleviate your boils?
Why not? It's rich in calcium and magnesium.

Do you think birds are born in trees
where they are nourished by sap,
or generated at sea from decaying wood?

Do you impute the occurrence of eclipses
to the irregular behavior of Kings?
Is the subconscious mind of the opposite gender?

Are old men's children seldom of good temperament?
Is melancholy an hereditary disease?

Does corruption derive from the father?

Does the death and resurrection of Jesus
repeat the legend of Adonis?

Can things divided
endure?

For the wicked, is there any punishment except contempt?
For the good, any reward but esteem?

Has a judge the right to sit in court?
Is Heretic a title of honor?
At the beginning, must Truth be labeled Apostasy?
I'd be interested to know what you think.

I?
Who am I?
It doesn't matter
does it?

Now for a few more questions. Tell me,
is a religiously dedicated populace
readily mobilized? Is war a total endeavor?
Do we yearn for the annihilation of our enemies
or not? To provide the deepest satisfaction
should the devastation be restricted?

Do human events exceed human understanding?

As we admit the possibility of a perfect circle
although none of us will ever see it,
do we admit the possibility of absolute good
however unlikely?

Has the Tree, symbolic of knowledge, been uprooted
and employed as the mast for a shipload of fools?
Have you studied the illustration for Josse Bade's
Stultiferae naviculae?

Oh, never mind! Let's sing and quarrel
and invent the past. Listen, my friend.
I'm a Knight, by name John Mandeville,
albeit unworthy, that was born in England
in the town of Saint Albans in 1322.
And I have had a map drawn to lead us
through diverse provinces beyond Persia
and Arabia and Egypt and Lybia until

we reach the land of Chaldea. Come along.
I'll take you to a city called Baghdad
which was named Sutis by Nebuchadnezzar
who founded it, where the prophet Daniel dwelt
and made the exposition of his dreams.

I own the books of Hermes Trismegistus
on which all things have been written.
You can read them, if you like.

I stole Kopernik's manuscript: *De hypothesibus motum
coelestium commentariolus*, which transforms the cosmos.
I'll tell you about it, if you consent to join me.
And pay no attention to those who call me a thief;
I respond to such accusations with Molière's phrase:
Je prends mon bien où je le trouve. How's a teacher's
eminence determined? By an account of his sources?

In works of the imagination is it necessary
for a creator to verify what he perceives?
Bruno formulated ideas concerning the universe
which were dismissed as absurd. That is,
until the development of spectrum analysis.

Lore of the world's not often expressed in rational terms,
my friend; and relations are bound by cabalistic logic
of their own. If you untangle this I'll feel rewarded.

Like the author of the *Song of Solomon*,
alleged to be an alchemical treatise
whose significance has remained an enigma,
I find it prudent to dress myself elusively
in a cloak of riddles.

The so-called Leiden and Stockholm papyri
unearthed not long ago in a Theban grave
contain recipes for the preparation of dyes
based on a text by Anaxilaos of Larissa
compiled during the first century B.C.
However, when the instructions were followed

they turned out to be utterly valueless.
It seems, therefore, that what we have are
the acrostics of some Egyptian alchemist
whose desperate search was as unsuccessful
as that of a few others I might name.

Mysterious wells of power lie within us,
but our odd inability to pump them
frequently leaves us discontented.
To do so, it's said, strike the bell,
light the flame, utter the iniquitous
formula: ABRAHAD . . .

The decomposition of a basilisk generates scorpions;
glass among stones is like a fool among men.
Wasps are conceived in the carcass of an ass;
beetles grow from the flesh of a newly killed horse.
Deadly poisons flourish in the bodies of women;
red is concealed beneath apparent wh . . .

Oremus.

Mary the Jewess was in fact Miriam, the sister of Moses,
a celebrated alchemist to whom we are indebted
for inventing the water bath, tribikos and kerotakis.

Succinic acid was initially described by Agricola,
benzoic acid first recognized by Nostradamus,
the existence of gases other than air by van Helmont,
disciple of Philippus Theophrastus Aureolus Bombastus
ab Hohenheim—a bit better known as Paracelsus.

Paracelsus. This irascible individual,
centuries before the Austrian analyst,
traced the origin of incubi and succubi
to somatically conditioned fantasies.
When he was appointed to the office
of Professor of Medicine at Basel
he publicly burnt the works of Avicenna
and Galen in a brass receptacle
to illustrate his contempt for orthodoxy,

as well as to notify the populace
that his doctrine was his own. And you?
Have you expressed such courage?

Avicenna, Abu Ali ibn Sina, by the age of sixteen
had learned so much about medicine that eminent
practicing physicians appealed to him for advice.
His *Canon* lists 760 drugs, including mandragora
and cannabis. He understood what we consider evident
at a time when nobody else imagined these things:
that phthisis is contagious, and soil and water
act as agents for the transmission of disease.
Studying physics, he predicated light's fixed velocity.
Mathematics, philosophy, music, transmutation, art
—everything everywhere stimulated his intelligence.
In brief, Abu Ali ibn Sina was an 11th century genius,
an undeniable testament to natural superiority.

Roger Bacon in the 13th century contrived a microscope
to study the nuclei of cells; 4,000 years earlier
at the court of Wang-ti some genius built a figure
with a metallic arm which always pointed south.
Well, everybody has a hobby. As the French say:
Chacun à sa marotte.

Chinese astronomers 500 years before Christ's birth
calculated the diameter of the solar orbit at 357,000 *li*,
a figure based on values derived from musical theory.
I mentioned this to my cousin, also an astronomer,
who replied that experiments conducted by Tycho Brahe
had enabled Kepler to introduce elliptical movements
for the planets—simple enough in a heliocentric order
but impossible if one insists upon geocentricity.
Thereafter, he continued, discovery upon discovery
followed Kepler's idea, ending centuries of stagnation
that originated in Chaldea. Indeed, my cousin said,
divinations such as those of Aristarchus and Scotus Erigena
developed all but accidentally from the roots of habit.
To be honest with you, I don't understand what he meant
but I do know our supremacy lies in the power to think.

Bishop Lightfoot, after laborious calculations,
announced that Creation occurred on the 23rd of October
in the year 4004 B.C. at 9 A.M. Archbishop Ussher
concurred with this hour but disputed the date.
Would you say their argument weakens my premise?

I admit to wondering why such diverse intellects
as Leibniz, Columbus, Petrarch, Newton and Tasso
accepted Catholicism. It's possible they resembled
those geographers who drew a continent in the south
where there was nothing but ocean and a few islands
because the absence of a land mass in that region
sufficient to balance the topography of the north
would leave the world lopsided.

Medieval skeptics wondered rhetorically
why God created iron just to forge nails
and thorns only to plait a crown. Why,
they inquired, did He fabricate a Universe
for the fabrication of a cross? Who knows?

Moslems visiting Frankish cities in the 12th century
were astounded by a repetitious parade of carved figures
depicting Biblical scenes on the capitals of churches.
They concluded that Christians must be idolators,
and referred to them with bottomless contempt
as servants of a piece of wood. Was this unreasonable?

Frederick of Germany, who led the First Crusade,
reputedly felt as comfortable among Byzantine ideals
and the precepts of the *Koran* as among those
of the Holy Roman Church. Few court scholars
could refute his logic or stand up against him
in the cut-and-thrust of metaphysical argument.
He spoke not only Greek, Latin, Spanish and French
but perfect Arabic. Erudite, and querulous, Oriental
philosophy was as familiar to him as that of Europe;
and what he liked best was to make fools of priests.
How the Church survived Frederick's accomplishments
is a proper topic for debate. The clutch of dogma,
tradition, fright—God knows.

"Your daughters must be Avarice, Lechery and Pride,"
the ecclesiastic Foulques de Neuilly remarked to Richard.
"I bequeath them to those that deserve them," quoth Richard.
"Avarice to the Cistercians. Lechery to the prelates.
Pride to the Templars." Summing it up: *Suus cuique mos.*
Everybody justifies his own point of view.

When they were young, Nizam al-Mulk and Hasan as-Sabah
swore perpetual friendship. A number of years later
Nizam was appointed Grand Vizier, while friend Hasan
founded the order of the Hashishiyun—from which
comes the word "Assassin"—whose first victim
was the Grand Vizier. Moralities vary.

Saladin, Salah al-Din Yusuf ibn-Ayyud,
slept uneasily one night, his dreams troubled
by the Old Man of the Mountains.
Three things were on his bed when he awoke:
a flat cake such as only the Assassins baked,
a dagger smeared with resinous poison
and a poem concerning death.

Contemporaries have described Saladin
as a sad-visaged little man with a gentle smile,
modest, chivalrous and profoundly cultured,
who could look past one's religion into his heart;
but after the True Cross had been captured
he fastened it to the tail of his horse
and trotted down the alleys of Damascus
ignominiously dragging Christendom's holiest relic
through dust and excrement. *Allahu akbar!*

Godfrey de Bouillon, walking barefoot
toward the Sepulchre after the fall of Jerusalem,
was accosted by a band of Crusaders who beseeched him
to appoint himself King; but Godfrey answered
that in a city where Christ was wreathed with thorns
he felt no desire to wear a crown.

What creature except Man
is cognizant of its limitations?

Pensée fait la grandeur de l'homme.

P-KR4.
P-QR4.

Dead conventions rot;
old cloth frays.

Chingis Cham, lacking food for his army,
commanded the soldiers to eat every tenth man;
Solyman the Turk, besieging Vienna,
heaped corpses higher than the city walls.

Not much changes.
Germans obliterate villages
and alter the course of rivers;
Americans as righteous as turgid penises
keep count over Asiatic bodies.

Listen. Monstrosities, miscarriages
and congenital anomalies are being reported
from Japan to Indochina.

Listen: "The over-ripe pear falleth in dung;
the rotted pear falleth into a slough."
Now tell me, how would this read in a mirror?
Vietnamese land suitable for agriculture
has been reduced by approximately 16%.
An area equivalent to Virginia, Connectic . . .

Father, I said, when the International Tribunal
reconvenes at Nuremberg who will be charged?
Atrocity, he said, which means inordinate cruelty
and recklessness, comes from the Latin *Atrox.*

Father, I said, on the news this morning
I heard of raids against the ancient Khmer temples.
My son, he said, can the depth or width of hate
be measured?

Father, I said, I came across three children
fused by napalm. The Lord's will be done, he said.

Father, I said, do you think I should keep a list?
Life goes past like the colorful pageantry of a dream,
he said. Look at it so long as God wills, however
it is not for us to judge.

Father, I said, let others practice clemency;
my purpose is to make sure the guilty aren't forgotten.
My son, he replied, determined effort is the cause
of perverted thought. Or is it the other way around?
Things are so easy to forget.

Hier sneuvelde op 7 Mei 1945 voor de . . .

A theater was constructed in Pangrac Prison
for the pleasure of high Nazi officials
who wished to observe unusual executions.
Now listen: it's only four miles from Weimar,
the home of Goethe and a German national shrine,
to Buchenwald. Or do you consider such associations
gratuitous?

Here's something else: a candidate for the SS
was ordered to murder his closest friend
and to crush the skull by stamping on it.
After that he might be eligible for initiation.
Furthermore, a curious absence of regret
has been reported among these people.

By the way, do you recall the name of the scientist
charged with developing the Nazi V-1 and V-2 rockets?
As you no doubt remember, he expressed disappointment
that there wasn't time enough to manufacture a model
capable of reaching the United States. Incidentally
would you happen to know where he lives? If so,
tell him his friend Simon Dubnow stopped by.

Unius dementia dementes efficit multos.
Lunacy feeds on itself.

Allied scientists learned that an atomic explosion
might be generated in one of three possible ways,
although nobody knew which would be most efficient.
Consequently, each of the methods was tested
and all three proved successful! I offer this
either for your amusement or, if you're like me,
for the obdurate exercise of your thought against it.

I've just been asked to name somebody I admire.
I admire the prudence of those deft brothers
McGeorge and William Bundy, whose ascent
flashed across bloody skies, counseling Mr. Johnson
most seriously, slipping aside the whirlwind
while others less gifted or perspicacious
stayed to argue.

I must admit I admire the preposterous agility
of Mr. Humphrey. What somersaults!

I look with humility toward the immaculate General
Maxwell Taylor, revealed against a blistering dawn
with unwrinkled trousers.

I listen respectfully to Pentagon spokesman Jerry Fr . . .

Oh, shit. Before counting half the lies
I could number every skull in Asia.

Disbelief, once sown,
flourishes in strange places;
true questions are answered
with greater ones.

We live in a world of indecipherable sin
and enigmatic punishment.

Pater nost...

Confined as it is to the depths of Redemption,
Christianity shows itself inimical to culture;
Lactantius points out that ignorance of geography
is meritorious and pleasing to God.

In Athens a decree was passed which forbade as impious
the study of astronomy. The first victim was Anaxagoras,
usually considered the greatest scientist of Asia Minor.

Ah-*hemm!* It's suggested that we evaluate the Athenians
not by their mistakes such as the execution of Socrates,
but by the fact that for two centuries they attempted
with some success to practice democracy. Well, first
let me refer you to Plato, and in the second place
to Xenophon—both of whom ranked Athens below Sparta.
Furthermore, never forget that a multitude of citizens
tend to be viciously wrong in their social prejudices.

It's worth remembering that we owe our few advances
to the consistent courage of minorities;
yet how is it that a truth affirmed every night
can be dismissed by morning?

How often have we been deceived by evil
wearing a virtuous mask?

Candidate Hitler addressing a Hamburg audience
in 1932 severely reminded the German electorate
that the streets of their cities were in turmoil,
universities were packed with rebellious students,
Communists threatened the nation not only from without
but from within, and the Republic's life was imperiled.
What was needed, he explained, was law and order:
Yes, without law and order our Nation cannot survive.
Elect us and we shall res...

Auschwitz-Birkenau: 2,000,000.

Hieronymus Bosch teaches that the world began simply
but was corrupted and lapsed into incurable madness.
We're obligated to believe him; to believe otherwise
would be madness.

Prophecies of medieval clergymen were vindicated
when flames brighter than new broken bones
uncoiled one summer above the Alamogordo desert
and humanity acquiesced in the assumption of power
by a nameless deity.

Hilka! Hilka! Hilka! Besha! Besha! Besha!
Hail, snow and fire mingle with blood!

Scholars speak of a parallel between Hiroshima
and the Hindu legend of Siva, who with a single shaft
simultaneously annihilated and redeemed the Universe.
I, mys . . .

It seems the President wishes to address us,
but why listen to paraenetical discourse?
Falsehoods flutter from his lips like moths.
If I heard him speak I'd waste my time
trying to squash them with applause.
Consequently I intend to go on and on
and on about my business.

A*hemm!* If you study a marble bust of Caligula
you can make out the features of an undergraduate.
I realize how surprising this sounds, but on my honor
I assure you it's so. And if you study Vespasian
long enough you'll see Lyndon Johnson.
If you doubt me, try it.

Listen, my friend. Augustus Casear
sponsored massive gladiatorial exhibitions
in which thousands demonstrated their lethal skills.
On Christmas—Christmas Day itself! United States bombers
sponsored by Tricky Dick attacked North Vietnam,
proving convulsively how little changes.
Lupus pilum mutat, non mentem.

Look, Jefferson rode to his Inaugural on horseback
with a saddlebag full of fossils he'd collected,
having been invited to speak on antiquities
before the American Philosophical Society.
No doubt you could equate this man with Nixon
or Johnson, although I wouldn't advise it.

Philodotus, I'm told, treated a depraved king
by ordering him to wear a crown made of lead.
Whether or not the treatment succeeded I don't know.
Rulers are notoriously intractable.

Perplexed, delirious kings should be fed *electuaries*
which are medicines mixed with honey or with syrup.
Sometimes they're called *eclegms*, but in either form
suggest a substance to be licked by the patient's tongue.

Aurum potabile is another splendid medicine.
This is a rich cordial alchemists concoct
with flakes of gold floating on its surface.

Mumiya or pitch, necessary for embalming, is beneficial.
Potions and ointments for wealthy patients are made of it
from the pulverized bodies of long-dead Egyptian nobles.

Hippomanes is the venomous humor of a mare in heat.
This is good for love philters.

It so happens that the foregoing prescriptions
are authentic, yet if you believe everything I say
you're a fool. You should learn to recognize
specious statements regardless of their source.
Now, listen attentively and attempt to decide
which of the following are true, which are false:

Animals did not eat one another prior to the Fall
of Adam.

It's possible to predict the future
by the coagulation of cheese,
and such divination is known as Tyromancy.

The name for Nightingale in every language
is melodious: *Nachtigall. Usignuolo. Ruiseñor, etc.*

Birds sometimes sing with deliberate artistry.

In the history of Art
the grotesque recurs constantly.

Responsibility for the execution of Socrates
must be shared by Aistophanes.

Clever men should be mistrusted.

Sacrificial victims are associated with planets,
which explains why the people of Haran dedicate those
with red hair to Mars.

Astrology is a minor branch of Natural Science
equivalent to the study of amulets
or physiognomy.

Funds for observatories look pitiable
compared to the coins astrologers scoop in.

Charlatans flourish.

Three is the most symbolic number possible.

All things desire the continuance of their being.

Man deceives himself with no trouble
yet he's unable to deceive water,
which is why those suspected of sorcery
are thrown into lakes and rivers:
the guilty drown, but the innocent fl . . .

Questions dart like shoals of glittering fish
or rise like birds wheeling in majestic harmony,
expanding and contracting in accordance

with the systole and diastole of the heart.
Answers? Keep them. I've got plenty.
In fact, I'll give you a few:

The women of Torreón weave songs with colored yarn.
False.

The brain of an East Indian is acutely sensitive to opium.
False.

Lemurians are unable to calculate or to reason
and live primarily by instinct. False.

You realize, of course, that I've been lying.
Now, if I can't be trusted after all this time
tell me, my friend, who does deserve your confidence?
Would you by chance trust the wind? On it goes,
unending, passing, never returning. But my question's
rhetorical. Let's try a few others:

The symbols of the USSR and of the USA
are the red rose of the Kremlin
and the white rose of the White House. True.

Bombs have rained on a jungle for 12 years. True.

By our unwillingness to object
we participate in senseless rituals. True.

The splendid dream has died. Probably true,
although the matter's disputed.

One of our Presidents will be remembered
for authorizing napalm. Perhaps.

A hideous beast slouched through Asia
in search of Bethlehem. This should be answered
by accomplished philosophers; nevertheless
if you're like me you have opinions.

The Antichrist was born in Chorazin.
I don't know; some say it's true.

The home of the Antichrist is Babylon
from which he shall emerge to devour the world.
This belief is popular. *De Babilonia coluber
exiet, etc.*

The Tarasque, a legendary beast
that lived on the banks of the Rhône,
ravaged the countryside until conquered
by St. Martha. Yes.

The fate of the Tarasque is central
to a Western world which eternally prays
and waits for the dragon's death.
Agreed.

The lamps of the Holy Sepulchre could not be lighted
on Easter Sunday of the year 1101, presaging ill fortune.
An established fact.

Coming events cast their shadows before.
Evidence is plentiful.

Mountains melt, stars fall, plague spreads,
earth vomits up its dead, skeletons come tumbling
helter-skelter out of tombs, and so forth.
Nobody questions this.

Supernatural communication
is characteristic of Catholic hagiography. That's so.

The Pope and Luther remind us of two whores
discussing chastity. There's not much room for doubt.

Who planned the Gothic cathedrals
or composed the earliest metrical romances
we have no idea; some eras pay little attention
to personal achievement. True again.

Work which is not ceremonial lacks sense
and meaning. Well, what do you think? I say
true.

Everything we undertake is a journey,
regardless of its nature, an attempt to recapture
one or two or three or four significant images
that have gained access to the heart.
I dislike the thought. False.

Whatever we succeed in doing
is the avatar of something at which we failed.
I reject this. No.

Innovative and visionary creations are not dissimilar
to the scribblings or paintings of psychotics.
I refuse to consider such a ridiculous hypothesis.

As to the following, I'll let you decide for yourself:
dialectical thought has little fear of contradiction
and revels in the ceaseless permutations of humanity,
whether in Hegel's system or in the *Mahāyāna*.

In the *Mahabharata* are exactly 100,000 couplets.
Count them.

The *Rig Vedas*, transmitted orally for 36 centuries,
preserve an accurate picture of the cities encountered
by Aryan invaders. Listen to them.

The Hindu goddess Kali is black because her name
comes from *kala*, which means black but also means time.
Therefore she is Time itself relentlessly licking up
Mank...

You should understand that this is not merely
a geometrical figure, but a musical progression
alluding to myth as well as to public and private
affairs simultaneously. Furthermore, each thought
requires its appropriate shape and dimension,
which has nothing to do with measurement.

You should understand the strength of thoughts.
A thought is capable of evoking its own atmosphere
around a subject, article, locality or concept.
If you are sensitive enough to detect the thought
you may be permanently affected.

Now, whenever we freely give a thing
to some other person we liberate ourselves
not just of that object but of the Self;
so we come to appreciate the essential emptiness
of all things perceptible to our senses.

Next, whenever we learn of a significant accomplishment
we seem to feel an imperceptible overflow from the deed,
as though it were streaming through space.

Parenthetically, although we employ "empty space"
at our convenience, you should know it doesn't exist
because starlight is omnipresent, filling the darkest
and furthest recess.

Several thousand celestial radio sources are known,
yet some of the most intense and persistent signals
emanate from regions where optical telescopes detect
nothing. Nothing! Do you hear?

We can look 4 billion light years into the past
but no further. Beyond that limit galaxies recede
faster than light itself.

It appears to us that Alcor and Mizar shine side by side,
although light traveling between them takes 3 months.

It seems to us that Antares, with a volume 60,000 times
that of the sun, must certainly be the largest star.
It isn't so.

Once upon a time we thought the sky must be egg-shaped,
revolving like a wheel as it carried the sun within,
and at noon the sun briefly rested on a point of the egg
—which explained why it looked smaller.

Well, what's been the purpose of this lecture?
To illustrate not just the lamentable inadequacy
of our senses, but the extent to which we misinterpret
"self-evident" facts. There might be divinity in our hearts,
but men's heads wobble and spin eccentrically.

Homer, unable to comprehend the fisherman's riddle,
was swallowed up by shame; Aristotle, incapable
of comprehending the motion of Euripus, drowned himself;
Democritus, in the hope of seeing clearly,
blinded himself.

So shut your eyes and tell me
if soldiers are accountable for what they do.

Tell me if Inquisitors act in accord with their conscience.

Are they happy whose history makes dull reading?
Is a revolt, once started, impossible to stop?

Do great voices go with meager wits?
Do majorities feed on slogans from the past?
Is every man's beginning prophetic?

Are such questions valid? I don't know.
Videmus per speculum in aenigmate.

For a time I went into public service
but my participation was marginal.
I rest apart from such involvement,
my brain as receptive as a darkened room
registering faint infiltrations of light.
people often denounce my sequestration
but why? Should I emulate others' lives?

If anyone asks how I came to be exactly what I am
I respond that I've had remarkable teachers,
none more so than my father. When I was a child
I liked to watch him wait on customers in the market
and I saw him weigh honestly to the 16th of an ounce.
After such a lesson how could I be different?

My most difficult lesson was taught by a Nahua poet
who warned me never to abase myself before a woman
like a dog before the person that feeds it.

I was informed by St. Bernard of Clairvaux
that love's waters flow less copiously
from the beloved than from the lover,
from the creature than from the Creator.

I've learned from Monsieur Arouet,
commonly recognized as Voltaire,
who built a church at his own expense.

Socrates, too, has instructed me.
Envious, froward and lascivious
by nature, being Socrates
he was able to correct himself.
My attempts to simulate him,
regrettably, fail. I don't know why
—unless I'm cursed with indolence
which is irremediable.

I'd be different, of course, if I were tall
and lean instead of resembling a terrier,
and if it weren't for this obvious birthmark.
But for better or worse, anatomy's destiny;
consequently, why should I be charged with events
or thoughts born of my beginning?

I hear myself condemned for selfishness.
I reject the accusation. What do we cherish most
from the world's stupendous spectacle?

Zoe mou, sas agapo.
My life
I love thee.

Perhaps you've been told about my wife.
If not, she suffers from a progressive disease
which is too disgusting even to talk about.

Some morning when she wakes up I won't be here.
I'm sorry, I assure you. And I justify myself
by pointing out that the paths of Munthe's garden
were designed to accommodate no more than one.

I have a friend, a Dramatist, who likens me to an actor
entering late in the action of a play, who thereafter
dictates how others respond, their movements
and the precipitant drop of the curtain.
Flattering, yes. But untrue.
Actually, who am I?
Listen. I'll be quite honest
for the first time since you and I met.
It may be pleasant to play the Fool, but in fact
my name is Dom . . .

N-B1.
B-R3.

I've been discussing life with my uncle
who finds the world a benevolent place.
Comfortable slippers, a fire, a cat
and a thimble of nutlike port.
Browning's his favorite poet.
Trahit sua quemque voluptas.

Last night I visited my sister, her husband
and their five children. Supper was splendid,
accompanied by popular tunes on the gramophone.
When I left she handed me a sack of fresh cookies,
kissed me on the cheek and expressed the hope
that I'd meet somebody who could make me happy.
Little chance. I remember too much too well
—the odor of dry-cleaned carpets, infant urine,
furniture polish and other such fragrances.
Outside their house an indifferent March rain
greeted me, and welcome. Requirements vary.

Thursday. What should I do? Totemistic objects
confront me: the mirror, symbol of self-knowledge,

a razor symbolizing knowledge of life that comes
through the consideration of death. What this means
is that I have two options. I'm free either to shave
or to destroy myself with myself as the audience.

To the wall beside my bed I've pasted a photograph
of the crystalline structure of chlorohydrate of heroin.
Presently I'll devour the flesh of God and lie here
waiting for my vision to expand.

Anxiety consumes me totally as a moth gnaws a garment.

Now it seems that Time is flowing back and forth;
if I try to lift a spoon my hand trembles.

My eyes in the mirror sparkle like twin drops of oil.

I come to myself in a high gold Renaissance chair
on some cool Italian loggia with marble pillars.
I gaze toward the sea. Suddenly my first wife
walks across the surface of the Mediterranean,
her hair dressed backward in the long cone of the East.
The indescribable majesty of her attitude reawakens
my profound esteem, and I understand that my life
must be almost over.

I am reborn a Spanish Dominican
scattering grain to pigeons in the courtyard
of an obscure monastery close by Zaragoza.
Mirabilia testim...

Is it not true that as we wish
we become?

Do you know who I was originally?
Do you know who I might be tomorrow?
Who was I tomorrow? Yesterday who will I be?

We aren't permitted to comprehend everything,
Horace writes, but that's not sufficient.

Dogs hear noises which are inaudible to us;
bats follow beetles through total darkness.
Cats look deeply into the infrared spectrum;
birds descry inner movement. And we must learn.
How can we endure ignorance? *Natura inest mentibus*
nostris insatiabilis quaedam cupiditas veri videndi.

Oh, there are many creatures with superior senses,
I'm often told. But in spite of their abilities
is any one of them life's custodian? Of course not.
None equals Man. He is born of generations of stars
gathered over billions of years. He is the glory
drawn from the spiral of the universe. His substance
is that of the sun. Have not all beings flourished
under his reign?

Speeches, I respond, flower magniloquently
from the heart's abundance.
Ex abundantia cordis os loquitur.

We are told by Friar Bacon that all in due time
vessels with one person to guide them will travel
faster than if manned by a hundred sailors!
Chariots without animals to draw them forward
will roll endlessly! Instruments for flight
will be constructed whereby a man at ease
may beat and subdue the air with wings
after the fashion of birds! Aren't the limits
set upon our credulity limitless? Friend,
listen: for the truth I'm your best bet.
Pay no attention to crystal gazers; nothing's
so firmly predicted as what's least understood.

Believe me when I tell you that earth is Heaven,
and we must strive to make it what it is.

Wouldst know how stars work upon us? They do
but incline; and if we be ruled by reason
what modest forces they command shall scatter
and dry up like summer snow. I swear it.

Aristarchus, who swore the earth revolved,
was denounced and jeered by Archimedes.
So you see truth's customary reward.

Do you believe Herodotus? His reputation is excellent
but let me tell you something. He wrote of a great voyage
around Africa by Egyptians during the reign of Necho II
six centuries before Christ, and claims these mariners
when they rounded the southern cape traveling west
beheld the sun on their right! Well, to be honest
I might have altered a few facts, but essentially
my indictment can't be challenged.

Claudius Ptolemy, the respected astronomer
of classical antiquity, taught that the Indian Ocean
was an inland sea because Africa curved toward the east
where it was connected by a land bridge to the Orient.
Now this instruction is strange because Alexandrian
explorers had established that Africa was circumnavigable;
and Alexandria, my friend, was Ptolemy's home! However,
we've been taught stranger things.

Columbus, having presented his case at Salamanca
to a council of academicians and theologians
heard it dismissed on the ground that common sense
as well as tradition proved the earth to be flat.
Furthermore, belief in the antipodes was heretical.
Intellectual progress since his day is problematic.

You may hear that prolonged concentration on a hollow globe
fatigues the optic nerve, facilitating phenomenal visions.

Some people will tell you that the life of the *mu*-meson
is extended as it nears the speed of light.

You're apt to be told that the saline plasma
which bathes our secret organs is little different
from the saline water of the sea; or that the world
drifts toward a region of the sky between Hercules
and Lyra. It's hard to know what to believe.

In school I was taught that antinopomancy,
which is divination by means of the entrails
of women and children, never fails; coincidentally
I saw the peaceable Mohandra Gandhi's corpse
conducted to his funeral on a gun carriage.
I stagger back and forth beneath a load of paradoxes.

People are measured by their clothes, I was taught;
sparrows don't live long because of their salacity.

Nightingales languish and die if another bird sings
more sweetly; lethal rains fall on the Orient.
Is either statement plausible?

The Pentagon may be mystically conceived
as a venomous turtle surrounded by its own excrement
while poisoned rice rots on the Vietnamese delta.
Can you separate these two?
I can't.

During the battle of Bannockburn when Edward II
was defeated, the arm of Saint Philanus,
ordinarily kept locked in a silver capcase,
escaped and was seen fighting. What do you think?
Regardless of your answer, how can you be sure?

Do you think insects see worlds of color
invisible to humans?

What's the purpose of dreams?
Some insist they permit us to go mad
with little danger.

Do we leave impressions of ourselves
upon objects that we've owned or touched?

Are the weeds green wherever jade is buried?
I've heard this is true because of humid exhalations
released by the stone, but I'm not convinced.

I do think an unexpected view of a crocodile
caused Artemidorus the Grammarian to go mad;
I believe that Apicus, having studied his accounts
and found himself to be worth 100,000 crowns,
destroyed himself for fear he might starve.
On the other hand, they say a Spanish soldier
in Yucatán sold three Indians for a bite of cheese.
I question whether anybody could be so foolish.

Mancio Sierra de Leguisamo, it's true, bet *El Sol*
and lost—a fabulous gold disk representing his share
of the Inca hoard at Cuzco. Perhaps I was wrong;
Folly's boundary falls below the horizon.

Men sometimes poison the flowers in their gardens
merely to deprive a neighbor's bees of honey.
Did you know this? It sounds fantastic, I admit,
but remember that hairs from the tail of a mule
ridden by Peter the Hermit brought high prices
as sacred relics throughout Europe.

You might also remember those devout German peasants
on the First Crusade obediently following a goat
and a goose toward Jerusalem. Here a curious analogy
manifests itself; but you should guess the parallel
without much trouble.

Nil agit exemplum,
litem quod
lite resolvit.
Quarrels open
and close unsatisfactorily.

Basilius, the Byzantine emperor, captured 15,000 Bulgarians
and blinded them, leaving one out of every hundred
with a single eye to lead the others home.
Could it be as some apostates claim
that our God is a hidden God?

According to the Seljuk Turks
Christians are polytheists

that kneel in front of images;
yet according to Christianity
the unbaptized will burn forever.
Can such arguments be resolved?

Do Christian concepts lead to the venal goddesses
of prehistory?

Is it worth knowing that death in the Iron Maiden
was decreed for such crimes as Plots Against the State,
Parricide and Disbelief?

Parricide, by the way, is a heinous crime
which is punished as follows:
the prisoner is stuffed into a goatskin bag
just large enough to contain his body
together with a dog, a viper, a cock
and a monkey. After the bag is sewn shut
it is borne on a skiff to the middle
of a lake or riv . . .

Eh? You don't believe that? All right, listen.
Here's a Spanish method. Dressed in a black tunic,
slowly accompanied by a procession of priests,
the criminal is escorted to the execution site
where he's seated on a scaffold and bound to the post
by an iron collar. Then a knob, manipulated
by a screw or lever, disloc . . .

Infinitely more subtle than Spanish priests,
British chaplains leading prisoners to their death
read aloud the Protestant burial service.

Why rake punishment from the past? Let me answer
without hesitation that overturned leaves reveal
historical detritus which might prove fatal
if ignored or suppressed. I consider it inadvisable
to forget, for instance, that at the Nottingham Assizes
in 1735 a deaf mute was pressed to death
for refusing to speak.

I think you should note that during the Inquisition
victims arrested by laymen of the Holy Office
were gagged at the first sign of resistance,
an ancient practice becoming rather commonplace.

It may interest you to know that the ground plan
of the Escorial resembles a gridiron
honoring the martyrdom of Saint Lawrence;
numerous courts represent the bars of the grate,
while the handle is symbolized by the palace.
Such an intricate and complex edifice
constructed *ad hoc*, as a memorial to suffering,
surely exhibits one aspect of human ingenuity
we would be unwise to neglect.

Knowledge is somewhat better than water,
I think, although both are tasteless and cold.
Love, on the contrary, is great and powerful.
Nonetheless, there are degrees.

I have read in the *Theologia Germanica*
that so long as a man loves parts and fragments
and above all himself, and holds converse
with them, and makes account of them,
he is deceived and grows so blind that
he knows good no more; for what is convenient,
pleasant and profitable to himself, and what is his
—these he holds best, and loves above all.
And because of this he never comes to Truth.

Within the compass of Hilton's *Ladder of Perfection*
which combines doctrine and private experience
together with sympathy for the requirements of others
we learn of three degrees in the contemplative life,
the first being knowledge of God and spiritual things
acquired by reason through various teachings
and a profound study of Scripture. Great scholars
after arduous effort reach this degree to some extent,
according to their intelligence and perseverance;
although we observe heretics, hypocrites and carnal men

acquiring such knowledge, who have never loved God.
The second degree consists of simple affection
without spiritual understanding, which often is found
among ordinary uneducated people who give themselves
liberally to devotion. At last we reach the third,
the highest form of contemplation to which we aspire.
Knowing and loving together are its components,
whose genesis may be felt, but whose consummation
God in His omniscience reserves until death.

Marvelous and stately is the place where the Lord dwelleth.

At Ephesus, in the year 431, Nestorius proclaimed a doctrine
emphasizing the human nature of Christ; now we hear this
as well as other ineluctable truths disputed on every side.
Explanations have been offered, yet none seems satisfactory.

On the third Sunday after Easter, May 8th, 1373,
for five hours, beginning at four in the morning,
Jesus Christ appeared to Dame Julian of Norwich.
Subsequent to this irresistible visitation
love's reality became the cohesive principle
and recurrent theme of her greatest comp . . .

Somebody interrupts to ask if there may not be situations
such as the present when men have neither time nor desire
to reflect on the ethical and moral implications of authors
whose text is reclusive. Ah, yes. Permit me to respond
elliptically. When the unfortunate revolutionary Zhelyabov
was tried for conspiring to assassinate Czar Alexander
he addressed these words to the court: "I was baptized
in the Orthodox Church but I reject Christianity,
although I acknowledge the essential teaching of Christ.
This essential teaching occupied an honored place
among my moral incentives. I believe in the truth and
righteousness of that teaching and I solemnly declare
that faith without works is dead and every true Christian
ought to fight for the truth and for the rights of
the oppressed and the weak, and even, if need be,
to suffer for them. Such is my creed." His little speech

echoes a somewhat earlier declaration of conscience:
Hier stehe ich, ich kann nicht anders. Luther, of course.

Somebody else poses a question: an ape made to suffer
in a laboratory for the future benefit of Mankind,
will it ever comprehend its torment? The inevitable
corollary being: is there another world beyond this
where human suffering has its answer? Ah, ah-*hemm!*
Let me suggest that you don't rely on consolations,
which tend to be useless; have no recourse to logic,
it seldom persuades. A determinate future appalls us
because our denial of Fate is weakened, and Free Will
accordingly withers. Is that clear? No?

Listen. Deities live among celestial interspaces
where they remain ignorant of human dissolution
because they themselves are constantly being renewed
by streams of atoms. We are unable to win their interest
through piety, or anger them either through neglect
or criminal activities. Deities live in perfect peace,
steadily contemplating nothing of greater relevance
than their own happiness. Do you understand?

I'll try just once more. During the 9th century
when divine union was regarded as conjunction
or as inhabitation in the soul of the mystic
Islam admitted only *ittiṣal*, or conjunction,
and violently rejected the thought of *hulūl*,
or inhabitation, because this approximates
Christian Incarnation. And for asserting *hulūl*
al Halladj, among others, was put to death.
Today we can't decide whether these victims
were heretics or martyrs. How difficult it is
to know God unless we're forced to define Him.

Religions often disappear with remarkable speed.
Documents pertaining to southeast Asia mention
Buddhism and Hinduism flowering among the Cham
of Annam from the 2nd until the 15th century;
yet only a few years after this kingdom collapsed
Buddhism had altogether vanished, while Hinduism

has by now disintegrated to such an extent that
its remnants are scarcely identifiable. In the West
Christianity's degeneration has proceeded so rapidly
and has so often been verified that to recapitulate
its disastrous course would be humiliating. Soon
history will say: *Consummatum est.*

I could recite a *chanson* in which Ralph of Cambrai,
having burnt a convent with all the nuns inside,
asks for a dish of meat. But his knights are horrified
because this is Good Friday. "Would you slay our souls?"
they ask. And he, being a pious man who could in no manner
offend his God, foregoes the dish. Incongruous, you say?
Haven't we heard the priests mutter, and watched their
grotesque gesticulations as they sanctify the weapons?

Benedicte! what dreamed I this nyght?

To praise without end or revile without purpose
is a habit of men in most of their undertakings;
yet praise or blame both ought to be measured
to ensure their readiness when we need them.
As Occam says: multiplication's not employed
gratuitously.

In my own mind I have examined many lives,
weighed them and judged them. And I conclude
they are imperfect—frail and discolored.
Human paths seem to me dark and obstructed.

Why is it, I have asked myself,
that I persist in setting myself
against the things that are?
I know life on earth to be wind,
that we are alive and swift,
yet done at the flip of a hand.

I know that each living thing suffers transfiguration.
I know that he who stitches an old love to his heart
encourages present grief.

I've heard that the more of love we've had
the greater must be our ultimate sorrow,
and if we could withhold ourselves from love
we could avoid pain. Great love for what we have,
great pain to be torn from it. Wife, child, riches
and whatever else is beneficial on earth must yield
more sorrow at its end than joy at its beginning;
all earthly things and love must turn to pain
—which is the end of love, as sadness ends joy
and revulsion always puts an end to pleasure.
This I'm told is life's course, and suddenly
to expunge what I feel out of mind and sense.
I know he's a fool who laments a mortal death
but what was taken from me cannot be replaced.
The insubstantial heart yearns to make of men
more than they are.

Habe nun, ach! Philosophie
Juristerei und Medizin
Und leider auch Theologie!
Durchaus studiert, mit heissem Bemuehn.
Da steh'ich nun, ich armer Tor!
Und bin so klug als wie zuvor.
I've studied theology, medicine,
jurisprudence and philosophy,
yet what good's it done?

In the Orient I was informed that the cicada symbolizes
reincarnation; and jade has the power to stop decay,
which is why people of the Shang and Chou dynasties
made use of it to seal the orifices of their dead.
Had I learned sooner I'd have slipped a jade cicada
between my wife's lips. Now it's too late.

I've been told that when a memory is intense
what's past becomes the future. If so, let it be.
I am small and afraid.

Who am I? Why do you ask? My face is
common enough, although people step back

uncertainly at my approach. I ignore them
and continue walking. Not much distracts me,
my eyes gaze inward. Six times around the world
I've gone, and God couldn't begin to guess
what I've suffered. I've told more fables
than Cagliostro, but as to my purpose
discover it yourself. *Lá vão os*...

Where the heart leads, we follow and counsel
and prevaricate with the tongue's thin leaf
From the innards of calves and partridges
we ply our conjurations.

Unlike Paracelsus, I have wandered across Europe
incognito, as eight complete personalities
disappearing with the danger of discovery.
Frogs in my belly go *Brecececex coax coax
oop! oop!*

There are those who call me a thief, a fraud
anticipating fortune, a journeyman, a hypocrite
and the Devil knows what. If it pleases you
to believe them, very well. For my part
I answer foolish speculation with silence.
My opinion of myself is what matters.
I think I'm neither the best nor the meanest.

I would say I resemble the King of Tsin at whose order
the Great Wall was begun, who decreed that every book
composed before his time be destroyed.

I would liken myself to the last Omayyid Caliph
Mutamid, whose consort Rumaykiija lay close to death
for the sight of snow-covered mountains,
who ordered a thousand almond trees planted
on the crown of the parched Cordoban hills
so their white blossoms might bring her pleasure.

In other words, approve of me or not;
inclinations vary. Where one door closes

another opens, as Cervantes rightly observes:
Donde una puerta se cierra otra se abre.

Only now I've begun to appreciate moments wasted
on disputation, unprofitable queries and intricate
subtilities. If I tell you that the bright stone
lapis lazuli must be washed exactly fifty times
before it's fit for use, would you spread the news?
Suppose I say that a Portuguese performing horse
was immolated because intelligence in animals
implies demonic possession, or remind you that
Paris was called Leucotia to honor the white thighs
of its women, how would you employ those facts?

If I should remark that in the Pacific depths
bubbles trickle ominously through concrete boxes,
what would you answer?

B-B4.
KR-B1.

Generations pass, stories change.

The Italians have a phrase: *Ogni vero non è buono a dire*
which seems appropriate. Don't tell everything you know.

There's a Latin expression: *Videant consules ne quid*
res publica detrimenti capiat. Let the consuls see to it
that the Republic suffers no harm. Thus conspirators
may be apprehended, judged and removed without delay.

Incidentally, I should point out a German fragment:
Wer fremde Sprachen nicht kennt, weiss nichts
von seiner eigenen. He who reads no other languages
knows nothing of his own.

Now, suppose we continue. For abolishing the traditional
habitaculum Dei Giordano Bruno was executed as a heretic;
yet if we consider that his hypothesis of other worlds
populated by human beings is still altogether speculative

the uneasiness he inspired begins to seem inevitable.
It was a contention of the authorities in Bruno's age
that ideas, like men, are apt to raise malignant children.
Does this sound familiar?

For having declared that Man created the Lord
instead of vice-versa, Liszinski was decapitated
and his body burnt, his ashes blown from a cannon.

For setting the Hearth of the Universe in motion
Aristarchus was accused by Cleanthes of impiety.

Roger Bacon rectified the Julian calendar,
devised a diving bell, spectacles, achromatic
lenses and the *camera oscura*, as well as proving
the chemical action of oxygen during combustion.
As you've probably guessed, he wrestled for his life
with ecclesiastics on the lookout for sorcery.

When a Crusader died his corpse was chopped up
and the flesh boiled away, after which the skeleton
could be returned to Europe for Christian burial;
but in the 14th century Pope Boniface issued a bull
interdicting this practice with the predictable result
that surgery was prohibited, and for years thereafter
scalpels could be used only by butchers, sow gelders
and executioners. However, a fullness of time comes
when reason dictates change.

The Council of Auxerre forbade offering sacrifices
to fountains or bushes. Even that's gone by the way.
Who knows what's next?

Apollonius of Tyana says there's no death of a thing
except in its appearance, just as nothing is born.
What passes from essence into nature seems to be birth,
as what passes from nature into essence seems to be death;
although nothing is originated and nothing perishes
but only now comes into our sight, and now vanishes.
By virtue of the density of matter it appears to us,

and disappears by virtue of the tenuity of essence;
yet it's invariably the same, differing to our senses
only in motion or condition. All is flux. *Panta rei.*

Chateaubriand collected and restored to their legitimate
position in the French language a variety of obsolete
expressions; I can do no less for ideas as stiffly faded
as allegorical tapestries.

Practically speaking, Saxo Grammaticus is impossible
because of a ponderous style. Then, too, his subjects
bored him—legends, heroes and a clutch of absurd gods.
Nevertheless, because he was a conscientious historian,
much unusual lore that otherwise would have been lost
has been saved. If asked, how many men could you name
who treat their trade with such respect?

Centuries ago Snorri Sturluson wrote a textbook for poets
in Icelandic so that they might recognize, correctly use
and exemplify the myths of human existence. These myths
have lasted longer than you think. Wednesday, for instance,
memorializes the god of hanged men Odin, customarily
represented with his tongue dangling. An image of him
nailed above a bed suggests the future to us today
as effectively as those yellowed cautionary skulls
posted by devout Christians in church niches.

Sometime early in the 17th century the *Codex Regius*
was discovered in an Icelandic farmhouse, and to it
we are obligated for most of our knowledge of medieval
Nordic mythological poetry. We read about giants, gods
and dwarfs confronting one another with riddle contests
and outwitting each other in tragic or comic battles.
One thing makes the stories impossible to forget:
time after time they end with a scene of destruction.
What we have, therefore, in these primitive tales
is an intuitive analysis of human behavior.

U.S. Marines invoking the "spirit" of a bayonet
sound as anachronistic as Scandinavian berserks

outfitted in wolf pelts—howling, yelping
and mouthing savagely incomprehensible cries.

Eadem, sed aliter. Schopenhauer explains:
The same things differently. History's motto.

Prisoners sacrificed to Xipe Totec gave up their skins
as well as their lives to Aztec and Mayan priests.
Although the custom seems rather repugnant
it's worth noting that this deity symbolizes Spring
when Nature clothes herself in fresh garments.

Spring invariably calls forth flowers,
those constant friends with whom we dine
and drink and dance. How should we live
without them? Their optimistic presence
encourages us. Their tidy profusion
surrounds us if we marry, and garlands
serve to christen our children.

Let me tell you about Mijnheer Busbeck.
When he was Ambassador to the Caliph
he got his first glimpse of tulips
and smuggled a few bulbs back to Holland,
which accounts for these exotic Asiatic colors
where we don't quite expect them.

Why it's appropriate for a beautifully gowned lady
to water a peony, no one can say; nor why a winter plum
should be tended by a monk. Why gardens are not swept,
however, is clear: to do so would disturb the fallen petals
which lie about carelessly meditating.

Butterflies, intimately related to gardens and flowers,
deserve their moment. But before discussing butterflies,
my friend, maybe you should move a little closer.
On a lurching carriage why choose opposite seats?
Someday it might be a pleasure to recall this moment.

Now, at the wedding of Jupiter to Juno
not only were the gods invited but many nobles,

among them a Persian Prince named Chrysalus
who came to the feast accoutered in bright robes
and accompanied by swarms of gay attendants.
Seeing him, several gods gave up their places
because they had judged him by his elegance
and thought he must be a distinguished guest.
Jupiter alone recognized him for what he was,
a light-footed fool, and transformed the Prince
and all of his sycophants into butterflies.
So they dip and flit about the summer long
in striped robes and we call them *Chrysalides*.

From flowers and butterflies we might as well proceed
to jade. *Pedra de mijada* in Portuguese, stone of the side,
because of its power to alleviate kidney ailments.
Yü is what the Chinese have named this precious stone,
identifying it as a treasure, and of its five virtues
the most edifying is that its edges, however sharp,
aren't meant for violence.

We might also discuss ceramics—a slight art,
yet an art of rare subtlety. Master ceramicists
couple true affection with assiduous training.

In a Nigerian museum a curious vase, a bronze vase,
was pointed out to me by a connoisseur who explained
that it was "Benin baroque." What's terribly amusing,
he said, is the artisan's exuberance. Just notice
here on the surface how a completely modeled torso
becomes abruptly two-dimensional at the waist
as though the figure had been squashed by a truck!
Not the least "primitif," it's a grand display
of the serious artistic intellect engaging itself
in a brilliant struggle with problems of form!
Having finished, he proffered a delicate cough.
I assured him I appreciated the instruction.
A connoisseur's amusements might seem a trifle
pallid; nevertheless, one does learn a little
no matter where one goes.

I'll not soon forget the *akrafokonmu*—that gold badge
belonging to one of the King's soul-guardians
who was expected to keep the King uncontaminated.
Here or there, apparently, men will prostitute themselves
to cleanse questionable deities.

Next we come to false objects. False objects
deserve discussion because of their variety
and prevalence: The most important fact about them
is that by their blatant and promiscuous charm
they excite the unwary. You must also keep in mind
that reproductions, forgeries, copies, imitations
and workshop pieces seem to glow by some remote
reflected light. Why? Because such dead things,
having no inner life, depend on the original.

Genuine objects are to be valued for the sensuous pleasure
they provide through color and shape, texture and design;
because of the evident skill that went into their making;
or because of an unusually high ideological content.
Once in a while all of these qualities occur together
and we then feel deeply rewarded. Secure in their merit,
genuine works wait for eventual cognition with dignity
and patience.

Perhaps I should mention that truly ancient bronzes,
those which have lain in the earth for centuries,
acquire a pure blue color like that of the kingfisher.
This might help you detect a fraud.

Ah-*hemm!* The preceding remarks on aesthetic sensibility
being a somewhat fly-blown and capricious digression,
let's continue from the transmogrification of a Prince
to a miserable King of Pontus named Mithridates.
Terrified of poison, he swallowed a dose every day
to insulate himself against future unpleasantness.
Allegedly, he devised an antidote containing opium
which later was elaborated into a complex prescription
by Nero's doctor, Damocrates. Several other ingredients

having been added by Andromachus, including snake meat,
the result was a cloying beverage—*Theriaca Andromachi,*
or treacle.

Etymology may bore you, but I like it.
Thus, although of no conceivable value,
I wish to tell you that the alarming word
"Saracen" is derived from the Arabic *sharkeyn*
by way of the Byzantine *sarakenos*—meaning
Eastern People—who are not, therefore,
by definition, at least, diabolic.

Khar sini is the Arabic expression for Chinese iron,
used in making mirrors which cure ophthalmic maladies
merely by gazing into them. But this peculiar metal
has another property esteemed by sensitive persons
as even more beneficial. If cast in the form of a bell
it rings with an unconventional sound.

Speaking of Arabs, those that sail from Port Sudan
to India each summer in marvelously decorated dhows
and return to Africa just before the autumn monsoon
have never heard of a sextant, and neglect the compass.
If asked by what method they determine their longitude
or plot a course, they are apt to reply: *Ana baref.*
This means that although they know, they can't explain.
Evidently a knowledge of India as well as of themselves
has been locked in their blood for generations.

Nauscopie, by the way, is the art of discerning
the approach of vessels from a great distance
or, being in a vessel, of predicting land.
We have no idea how this phenomenon operates
and investigation reveals only one practitioner,
a Frenchman named Bottineau who developed it
to a high degree on the island of Mauritius.
Questioned about this exceptional power
he responded with greater sophistication
than an Arab sailor, but what he said was
essentially the same: he wished to be excused

from giving an account because mere possession
of a talent ought to be considered sufficient;
one ought not also be expected to def . . .

Someone wishes to know how we escape Intellect's
crippling fallacies. Let's just say, as Blake did,
that one either devises one's own system or is enslaved
by another.

Now, if you'll wait till I peel away my red moustache
we can discuss Bijugos carving, mastabas, indestructible
monuments, theoretical physics, Etruscans and vagabonds
as well as those who are always poor—Earth's quiet ones.
My name, if you've not yet guessed, is Theophrastus
and I've been everywhere in the world. Friend, there's
plenty I could tell you. Plenty!

Once you've watched lepers crawl through Hyderabad
nothing else matters. What significance those bodies hold
will manifest itself, I assume.

Once you've heard the affluent whistle of bombs
while tasting hunger night after night
you start to understand about tomorrow.
Plus ça change, mon ami, plus c'est la même.

Wherever the teleidoscope barrel turns
we observe distracting sights. Yesterday,
for instance, the police shot my brother.
The coroner picked 28 bullets out of his corpse
before going to lunch. The mayor, bless him,
has ordered an immediate investigation;
and we look forward to being told exactly
what all of us know, having heard it
so often: the police were not at fault.
Whether or not you agree with my analysis
can be predicted by the cut of your clothes.

Seasons pass and stories change, I've told you
at least twice: *Eadem, sed aliter.*

Would you say the earth revolves on its axis?
You would? If so, how does a terrestrial component
such as a cloud move across the globe's surface
while the globe whirls in the same direction?
Hypotheses are simple, as you see; answers aren't.

The carcass of a Saint won't stink, they'll tell you,
which is taken as positive proof of its curative power.
If you swallow that you're just the sort they need.

If you boil a crow's eggs and put them back in the nest
the crow will fly to the Red Sea and return with a stone
which magically restores the eggs to their natural condition.
Believe it or not, as you like. I don't. Day after day
I've heard the news.

Despicable crimes must be dealt with realistically,
according to Mr. Hoover; and the situation progresses
satisfactorily in Asia, according to General Abracadabra.
Huh! Hang a toad from your belt to escape the plague.

Listen. During the summer Diogenes wallowed in hot sand
but when winter came he embraced frigid statues. Why?
Because things happen that cause us to lose our senses;
if not, we've none to lose.

They say the melancholiac occupies himself with reflection
while the maniac's head is stuffed with impetuous thoughts.
As for myself—ah, that depends. I've addressed oak trees,
occasionally taken scissors to my clothes, robbed, burned,
raped and diddled a gullible populace. At other times
I've adamantly refused to open my mouth for a week.
My wife's convinced I've made a captive of myself,
immured myself in a singular dungeon. What she forgets
is the freedom to indulge one's dreams.

Strangers mistake me for Agrippa von Nettesheim
but he died with his face pressed to the earth,
the devil's disciple. There's the difference.
We're alike in several ways, I admit. I, too,

have dabbled in alchemy and occult practices,
argued for argument's own sake, mistrusted
the science of pure Reason. I've said my name
is Theophrastus. And believe me, I know everything.
You'll have trouble finding a better teacher.

Some people reward my services with a few florins,
others pretend poverty. The decision is yours.
In either case, welcome. I'd sooner see you poor
than ignorant. *E meglio esser mendicante che ignorante.*

Now, how should one answer propositions concomitantly
imaginable and preposterous? It has been suggested,
for example, that radio messages from other civilizations
may have been falling on a heedless earth for centuries,
apprehended by insects, lizards and fish—obviously
an absurd situation.

The very fate of nations might well be determined
by Mercury's magnetic fields, or by electron density
around the moon. Possible? Ridiculous?

Olaf Stapledon wonders if the galaxy might be evolving
toward consciousness. What do you think?

Astronomers have detected a radiant jet of light
shining with inconceivable strength from the nucleus
of Messier 87. The jet's length is hundreds of light years,
its energy equivalent to that of a million supernovae.
A natural light of this magnitude seems inexplicable,
but that it could be contrived by sentient beings
attempting to communicate with others is ludicrous.
We're troubled by these enigmas we discover in Nature
and in ourselves, and would like to understand.

Few of us have experienced freedom from gravity,
yet it remains oddly familiar in dreams.
Explanations have been offered; none seems adequate.

In a dark quiet room even the most equable man
begins to feel isolated, and after a while goes mad.
Why is this? Do we feel such affinity for others?

Dr. Simon Remo postulates that our principal pursuit
will become the expansion of intellect by electronics.
Progress accelerates, to be sure, feeding on itself;
knowledge doubles every decade and already twenty years
of school prove wretchedly insufficient. Beyond that
we agree on precious little.

Maybe you're acquainted with those spidery bronze pontiffs
modeled by Floriano Bodini from whose voluminous cloaks
multitudes of wooden doves escape—a concept blasphemous
yet paradoxically truthful. So we see ourselves confounded
by cryptograms dense with a stringent purgative logic.

Listen. The Archbishop of York, Dr. Cyril Garbett,
approved the manufacture of hydrogen bombs;
but in the *Mahabharata* we read: *Do naught to others
which if done to thee would cause pain.*

Listen. A disciple of Gautama Buddha walked on water.
The Enlightened One himself had a virgin mother,
performed miracles, was transfigured, fed 500 people
with a single cake, and so forth. How unremitting
and very powerful must be the forces that undo us,
and divide an annihilate our mutual religion.

A rabbi named Bachï cast the horoscope of Jesus;
yet why should this solicit the condemnation
of Christians everywhere? We're reduced to bewilderment.

Why would no man read what Jesus wrote on the ground?

On the island of Patmos to which he had been exiled
by Domitian, John received the book of the Apocalypse.
Why did a merciful God command him to eat its pages?

The art of silent reading was conceived in 384 A.D.
by Ambrose, the bishop of Milan. One of his disciples,
later known as St. Augustine, was grievously distressed
by the sight of a man reading without making any noise.
We hear ourselves ask what difference it should make.
Indeed, there's no end to our plaintive queries.

The old priest thinks I'm a recalcitrant child,
a lamb lost. I avoid him because I can't trust him.
I have no faculty for entering alien theologies
and very little wish to be buried by his custom
with my feet pointing toward the Holy City.
Why should I get up if a Redeemer approaches?
Frankly, I question the possibility of solace;
so permit me to die as hopelessly as I was born.

As I grow older I consider myself less in agreement
with Plotinus that only in a world beyond
does the true object of our love exist
with which we may unite ourselves—of which
we can have some part, and intimately possess.

Now I think I'll wake you up. Tell me,
what's love? Ah! Everybody replies at once.
Why do I hear nothing worth remembering?

According to St. Maximus, what a man loves
that he assuredly clings to; and everything that obstructs
his way to it he despises, lest he be deprived of it.

Look. Here's one sort of love: Jean Fouquet,
commissioned to paint the King's mistress, Jeanne Sorel,
depicted her as the Virgin Mary with an aureole
of angels.

Here's another: Evagrius of Pontus
claimed when he lay dying that for three full years
he had gone untroubled by fleshly desire,
after so long a life of toil
and ceaseless devotion.

Not that I repudiate his claim;
however, personal experience demonstrates
that intense intellectual passion drives lust out
at least as soon, and thoroughly.

Miguel de Molinos, on trial in Rome,
defended his strange sexual obsessions as sinless
purifying acts which, continuously effected by the Devil
and passively permitted by the interior Christian,
providentially deepen one's repose in God.
As you might guess, he was imprisoned;
but the charge was Heresy!
Mirabile dictu!

Men speak of a miraculous "voice"
that distinguishes between real and fluctuating
right and wrong; yet all too seldom
do we witness demonstrations.

The progress of the Soul toward sanctity is threatened
by multifarious temptations.

Much as physicians introduce some very bitter herb
to cure the body, God in His omniscience
introduces trials to purge men of their habits.

Acquaintances wonder if I'm not atheistic.
I point out that I've examined wooden wounds
and painted ulcers on the statues in Valladolid;
furthermore, I've touched the hand and occipital bone
of John the Baptist in Constantinople. If anyone asks
why I refuse to enter a church—well, I just say
it's degrading to genuflect before abstractions.

I've assiduously studied the dominant religions
and have learned that whereas some establish Creation
in the quite recent past, no doubt anticipating
the imminent destruction of the universe, others
not only look back through unspeakable vistas of time
but forward to still greater ones. Hinduism, for instance,

would exemplify the latter, Christianity the former.
Which suits you best depends on your temperament.

If one characteristic predominates in Christian theology
it would seem to be a gross tendency to assimilate.
From Mithraism the eucharist was ceremoniously stolen,
as well as a midwinter festival on the purported
birth date of a "savior," and the concept of baptism.
Holy water, incense and the morbid cross of Golgotha
are adaptations of pagan instruments, just as Priapus
with his tremendous organ pops up as St. Guignolet,
patron of sterile women.

Chaldea, says Berosus, was ruled by ten antediluvian
kings for several thousand years; legends of Iran
commence with the reign of ten Peisdadien kings
—men of the ancient law who lived on *homa*
or nectar, and preserved their sanctity. India claims
nine Brahmadikas, who, with Brahma their founder,
make ten, who are known as the Petris, or Fathers;
ten emperors ruled over China, partaking of divinity
before historical times. Germans speak of Odin's
ten ancestors, just as Arabs believe in ten kings
of the Adites. So, when we read of ten antediluvian
patriarchs in the Book of Genesis we recognize them
at once. What distinction Christianity does possess
we would expect to find not in its origin or structure
but in the moral purpose, which might be superior.

On the 7th of June, 1099, an army of Crusaders appeared
beneath the walls of Jerusalem, this city which had been
for such a long while the substance of their dreams.
But it was a disappointing place, and many were amazed
and asked why the Lord should have chosen a useless plateau;
nevertheless, assisted by angels, they boldly set about
breaching the gate in order to behold a new Heaven
and earth where the poor and the just would reign forever
in a city flowing like a fountain with indescribable riches.

Visitors to the Church of the Holy Sepulchre in Jerusalem
are expected to buy a candle before entering the whitewashed
cell for a look at the sarcophagus. That's just a start.
Pound notes, dollars, *pesetas, deutsch Marks, francs, lire*
and many other kinds of money cover the cracked marble lid.
Saint Augustine observes that we would rather see gold
than the sun itself. He's right, I think. When I was there
three American nuns were kneeling to kiss the sarcophagus
while a priest busily arranged and rearranged the blanket
of banknotes. *Dove l'oro parla, ogni lingua tace.* Italian
or not, you get the idea.

To be honest, I confess I haven't visited Jerusalem;
however, you must keep in mind that the magus seldom
concerns himself with fact. He makes use of falsehood
when necessary to serve his ends. Furthermore, everything
I've told you about gold happens to be the truth.
Our very nature ebbs and flows with this commodity.

In Saladin's treasury when he died were 47 Nacerite
dirhems and a single Syrian gold piece. He owned nothing,
left nothing and coveted nothing. He had no houses,
furniture, gardens, plowed land or property of any sort
and money floated like a ribbon between his fingers.
Whatever chanced to come his way he distributed,
gracefully permitting himself to be exploited
and swindled. How foreign he sounds.

Beha ed-Din, attending a military conference
at which Saladin was present, remembers hearing him
ask several times for a drink of water. Neither his voice
nor his manner was imperious, with the result that servants
neglected him. It's difficult to understand exceptional men
because so much needs consideration.

When an argument broke out among Frankish barons
as to whether Ascalon or Tyre should be sacked
the problem was resolved by writing both names
on scraps of paper and offering them to a child,
who obediently chose one. So Tyre was besieged

and reduced to starvation—eventually capitulating
on the 7th of July, 1124. All things have their place,
it's said, if we but knew how to place them.

The first German army trying to reach the Holy Land
was massacred in 1101, the second in 1147. A third,
led by Frederick of Hohenstaufen, called Barbarossa,
got past the Turks and apparently was well on its way
when Frederick went for a swim in the river Cydnus,
caught cold and was dead in a week. Almost at once
his entire force disintegrated. Some few commanders
straggled back to Europe while others rode uneasily
toward Antioch where they ended up in the slave market.
Frederick's embalmed body decomposed in the heat
—his gummy bones marking the end of Teutonic hopes.
It seems the German's aren't fated to reach Jerusalem.
Idealistic armies from other nations have done better,
if not much.

Deo duce, ferro comitante.
With God as our leader and sword . . .

Lat. 12.10 s.; Long. 114.31 e.
The wind has changed. It blows ominously
out of Asia. We petition the Captain
to alter course, but he replies:
"Only those who do nothing make no mistakes."

Petrels. Small sticks. Currents flow against us.
Whales and porpoises, creatures of infinite promise
playfully ride our wake. The sea's static environment
demands little more than nominal intelligence.
With men it's different, and unspeakably bitter.

Friday. Much talk of a jinxed bark on her maiden voyage
with a ballast load of rubble from a graveyard.
Some pray, others curse.

Gulls wheel overhead, crossing
and recrossing.

Presentiments, omens.
The compass drifts like a toy;
fiery branches drop from the overcast
not six leagues ahead. The time is full of evil.
We wait and watch, yet all we can establish
is that we have been born part of the Universe,
our weak voices mean nothing to those that control us
and back and forth we travel helplessly.

Since yesterday a good thirty leagues, we're told,
but contradictions strangle us like Sargasso weeds.
Does the Captain keep a second log for his own purpose?
He has set himself, some think, out of his mad obstinacy
to proselytize and subdue a thankless continent.
Measuring the Indies would be less foolish.

The mate tells of a New England whaler
that seized and carried off a group of savages
from Easter Island. Three days out they leaped overboard
meaning to swim home. Sorts and degrees of madness.

New Year's Day. This morning sighted a sun-bleached longboat
with a skeleton slumped at the bow dressed in tatters
of an officer's uniform with square brass buttons,
faded epaulets and gold-braided hat. No papers
nor any name. There was little we could do,
so we sailed on. Few dared look back.
Put to sea if you'd learn to pray.
Se queres aprender a orar,
entra no mar.

N-K3.
Q-Q1.

Midnight. Thought of my wife,
played the flute.
Life's a befuddling pilgrimage.

Scorpio will rise above Europe
13,000 years hence, I've heard.

But proof's a long time coming.
So much we take on faith,
charged like an eel with doubt.

The world was created from a watery void,
we're told, by the Mayan forefather gods Tepeu
and Gucumatz, who endowed it with animals and plants;
but manlike beings they had fashioned out of mud
returned to mud, and wooden figures they built
were destroyed, and the first men created from flesh
were wicked and drowned when black rains swept the earth.
Not until this flood subsided, so the story goes,
did our ancestors come to stay. Maybe gullible Indians
believe such legends. I don't.

Peruvians insist that the first Inca, Manco Capac,
and his sisters were created on the Isle of the Sun
in Lake Titicaca. This is absurd, yet one thing
about the Incas sounds unpleasantly familiar:
they thought they were the Sun God's favorites.

It's been suggested that the Incas might have been
descendants of Armenians, Egyptians, Chinese, Welsh,
the lost tribes of Israel, or the sons of Kublai Khan.
Walter Raleigh persuaded himself that Manco Capac meant
Ingasman Copac—a bloody Englishman. Whoever they were,
we know from Spanish chronicles that these sophisticated
ambitious people obliterated every previous civilization
by what we call the selective manipulation of history.
Pedro Cieza de León inquired in 1549 about the ruins
of Tihuanaco, but nobody could tell him a single fact
about the people who had built this important city.
If you go there now all you see are a few pillars
and lintels—empty doors opening toward nothing.

On the windy plains of Mongolia, nearly obscured
by centuries of drifting soil, one blunt stone post
marks the site of Karakorum, Genghis Khan's capital.
But the stone stands there with indescribable force,
as though concentrating on his terrible passion.

Where the heart wills, the feet follow.
Lá vão os pés onde quer o coração.

Prince Henry set up his court at Sagres
on a remote headland in a corner of the kingdom,
eager to learn what lay outside the boundaries
of contemporary charts—despite assurances
from celebrated topographers that the ocean
poured madly over the lip of the world
in a roaring cascade. Henry the Navigator
he's called, whose dreams sailed out of Sagres.

Alexander built 12 altars to mark the limits
of his conquest; Eratosthenes, less easily satisfied,
calculated the circumference of the earth.

Ptolemy decided to collect information in books;
Asoka urged his people to construct hospitals,
educate women and cultivate herbs.

Auzout contrived the filament micrometer;
Supputius traveled across Europe
to speak with a wise man and returned
despondent, without having talked to anybody.

Von Humboldt, after visiting Colombia and Venezuela,
needed 80 volumes to describe his marvelous experience.
I've read von Humboldt's entire account, by the way,
except for the last volume—which I'll never read
because I don't like things completed. However
what I want you to appreciate and contemplate
is the infinite complexity of our mosaic.

Ventris prepared for destiny at the age of six
by teaching himself Polish. Later, I've heard,
he was able to see Minoan linguistic structure
under the patterns and signs of Linear B as clearly
as an architect looks through balustrades. This ability
to recognize a method within apparent confusion
is characteristic of all competent men,
but is more pronounced in genius.

My uncle, himself a famous cryptographer,
told me that the value of the alphabet's second letter
was 2 while the first had a value of 1, the third
had 3 and the eighth had 8. After telling me this
he asked how much I understood. I replied
without a pause that he had spelt Bach.
Then he said these total 14, which if inverted
reads 41, signifying J. S. Bach who dictated a line
with 14 notes while on his deathbed:
Before thy throne I now appear.
All in all, he continued, in the melody
41 notes occur, and such symbolic utterances
abound in the compositions of Bach.
But as to their purpose,
beyond his obsession with symmetry,
we have no idea. Dear Uncle, I said, reality
to some of us is anathema. Now may I play you a trifle?

The members of my family can't guess what I'm up to.
If your relatives are like mine you know what I mean.
I answer their questions by saying Delius raised a shutter
against the world, I've done the same and leave it at that.

Suppose we go back a moment. Archimedes of Syracuse
was at work on a mathematical problem when a centurion
stood in his light. The celebrated thinker objected
and the soldier responded by murdering him. Well,
I've forgotten just what this was intended to illustrate.
The tumescent stupidity of soldiers has been so thoroughly
docum—Ah! Here we have it: *Noli turbare circulos meos.*

Next, the question arises
as to where one starts measuring a circle.
Have you any idea?

Why are the stars unequally situated?
Nature is equal in all things,
always proportionate and constant,
assigning just dimensions to everything
including the sapient face of Man
where much corresponds. Therefore

why should not this be true of the sky?
which is the loveliest of Her works.
Why are the Heavens irregular? Tell me
whence comes such difference?

Why does Africa breed so many venomous beasts
and Ireland none? Athens owls, Crete none?
Why are Spaniards white, and Italians,
yet inhabitants of the Cape of Good Hope
blackamoors, equidistant from the Equator?

If the earth be 21,500 miles in compass, its diameter
be 7,000 from us to our Antipodes.
What shall be comprehended in all that space?

Why is it that if you ascend to the top of a high hill
in America you will faint? Some say for lack of thick air
to refrigerate the heart; but I don't know if I'd agree.
Nor would I avow that Jupiter's two monstrous eagles,
which he let loose and told to fly to the world's end,
met at Delos. There is very little I can be sure about
and I think too much of consequences.

Why did 120,000 lose their lives at the siege of Ostend?
Why were 1,000,000 slaughtered at Jerusalem?
How many corpses should we count, and for what
cause, in Vietnam? Scaliger claims we leave our battles
as testaments to madness for succeeding ages.

It's alleged that for lack of another world to strike
Alexander wept; and at the sight of enemy corpses
heaped ceremonially in front of his battlefield tent
Colonel Patton's face showed undeniable pleasure.
Could you account these men mad? To what degree?
Don't forget, the earth wallows like a whale in blood
and a man's attitudes are inherited from his father.
Differently put, opinions vary. Some openly praised
Alexander, although Seneca called him a bedlam fool;
nor is popular judgment of our leaders unanimous.

The Brigadier General accused of shooting children
from a helicopter was examined by a jury of his peers
and found to be above reproach. Their interpretation
points out that the general was directing fire against
figures taking evasive action. Such verdicts, some argue,
exemplify and constitute a secondary madness far more
malignant than the original. About all we can remark
with certainty is that dissent rules.

Colonel Giteau regards it as a fundamental error
to distinguish between soldiers and civilians.
Say he's right, the quickest route to *Einwelt*
must be across the bodies of all who oppose us.

Belzec: 600,000.

Vrijdag, 9 October 1942.
Als het in Holland
al zo erg is,
hoe zullen ze dan
in de verre en barbaarse streken
leven, waar ze heen
gezonden, worden?

So many were murdered and buried in fields
around the Birch Forest that the soil grew marshy
from the putrefaction of their bodies.

Listen. The Psychological Warfare Section of SHEAF
has compiled a 13-volume report on the Nazis
which concludes that automatism and absolute obedience
had been firmly established throughout the country.
Gone was all presumptive thought of questioning
either one's superior or the national policies.

Now listen: because he refused to cooperate
with a Congressional subcommittee investigation
of what's referred to as "premature anti-fascism"
my brother-in-law has been cited for contempt
and is spending a year in Atlanta federal prison.

I managed to talk to him as they led him away.
I asked why he'd challenged the authorities
and he said someday his children would be grown
and would ask how he had registered himself
against these lunatic times. Congratulations
on your courage, I replied, although your logic
is fallacious. Your children won't be interested.
It would have been enough to respond as Sièyes did
when asked in what fashion he conducted himself
during the Reign of Terror. *J'ai vécu*, he said.
I lived through it.

Sir Richard Grenville was so enraged by the Inquisition
that he chewed wine glasses. Not that it did any good.

Frère Jacques Clément, assassin of Henry III,
as tormented as the Englishman and mad with rage
composed this anagram with the letters of his name:
C'est l'enfer qui m'a crée. Do you understand?

What I'm getting at, of course, are the consequences
of despotism. Ecclesiastic or secular, it's the same.
Submission to the mindless planets of authority
generates delirious belief, entertains hallucination
and stuffs our heads with horrifying compromises.

Santayana, the philosopher, warns of a long winter
approaching—one of those seasons which periodically
overtake civilization. We might argue; nevertheless
bleak signs blow across the wind.

First. Aramaic, the tongue spoken by Jesus
has not been heard for 12 centuries.

Second. In the Jura Mountains a nightingale
fell asleep on a vine and awoke to find tendrils
coiling around its feet.

Third. Although spring will soon be upon us
no buds have appeared.

Fourth. My teleidoscope looks inward.

I could continue placing particular beside particular:
in the Mexican state of Colima an ancient tomb
was opened, revealing the ceramic effigy of a dog
wearing a human mask; in the New Guinea jungle
a wrecked World War II *Boomerang* was discovered
with its pilot waiting patiently at the controls;
in France a severed head looked up at the blade,
cognizant of what had happened; a bacteriologist
in England died of a foul disease he invented;
in America 49 million dollars was appropriated
to study the idea of housing apocalyptic missiles
in the North Dakota mountains. *Pater noster, qui*...

You know that radiostrontium is analogous
to calcium, but do you know what this means?
It means radiostrontium can substitute itself
for calcium while bones are being formed.
This, in turn, means that every child born
during atmospheric tests of atomic weapons
carries in his bones—not just temporarily
but like a hallmark stamped on a chalice
a malignant gift from the AEC. Comment or not,
as you wish. Your response will be evaluated.

According to the present state of theoretical physics
energy and matter both are regarded as indestructible,
undergoing perpetual modification—one into another
and back into itself—each changing its manifest form
yet never ceasing to be; much like the routes men take
which divide, circle and constantly intersect.

Léon Bloy thinks we are the words, letters or versicles
of a magic book; I say we could be likened to sleepers
who shout and tremble in our sleep, or perhaps to fish
which toss and roil the shallows.

Have you guessed my name? Louis Claude de Saint-Martin.
Hopelessly incapable of distinguishing a plaintiff's

claims from those of a defendant, I exchanged the law
for military service. Not that I cared to be a soldier
but barracks life promised leisure to pursue my studies
of philosophy and religion. You'll be good enough, I trust,
to excuse me for having withheld my identity. Regardless,
I should like to tell you that all of us are defined by
three transcendental experiences: sexuality, aesthetics
and violence.

To be quite honest, I am Prince Mourschid of Schaizar
and above all I treasure excellence. Hours I spend copying,
then joyously recopying the *Koran* in graceful script.
I wish to tell you that for the sake of truth men endure
mockery, calumny and abuse too vile to be remembered.

I confess to deceit. In fact, I'm Pope Gregory VII
and I've been obliged to take up residence in Salerno
because of an Emperor whose name is not worth mention.
I have loved justice and despised iniquity. As a result
I must live in exile. But what I think you should know
is that influential mystic writing often assumes the form
of homily. Reproof or solemn discourse on moral conduct
demonstrates how fashions change.

Actually, I'm a scholar in Erasmus' *Dance of Fools.*
The past, let me remind you, is indestructible
and all things return.

In reality, I'm Simon Dubnow addressing you
from the grave. I've begun to feel a little anxious.
I'm afraid you might forget. Tell me, what's happened
to Lyndon Johnson, Rusk, Rostow, Bundy, McNamara,
Westmoreland and the others. Have they escaped?
Tell me, my friend, how goes it? *Wie geht's?*

Peace, Dubnow. While paper lasts
where can they hide?

QR-B1.
P-N5.

God accompany you
to the last milestone
and beyond. *Dhia Bith leat
chun an ath Chlach Mhile agus n'as . . .*

It's said that not long after the Crucifixion
a man who had never seen death made his way to Asia
where he founded a huge and puissant Christian kingdom.
Some people believe this man was John the Baptist
while others say he was Our Lord's favorite disciple.
All we know is that someplace in Asia he still reigns,
untouched by age, and calls himself Prester John;
and most of us would surrender everything we possess
for the privilege of entering his settlement.

Arabs think we crisscross the world like camels
in the hope of fulfillment. For instance, Ibn Batuta
left Tangier on a pilgrimage to Mahomet's birthplace
and the Tomb of the Prophet. In Mecca, as prescribed,
after 7 circuits of the Kaaba he kissed the black stone;
but then instead of returning to Tangier he traveled
further and further—wandering and meditating
for 29 years. What he thought about we have no idea,
but in those years he must have seen many wonders.

Hsüan-tsang, a Buddhist monk and 7th-century scholar,
deeply troubled by discrepancies among the sacred books
decided to go traveling through the West, where with luck
he might meet a man wise enough to answer his questions.
Although the Emperor had denied permission for his trip
he set out, encouraged by a dream. At the Gobi Desert
his guides became frightened and refused to continue,
so Hsüan-tsang went on by himself, following a trail
of camel bones to Hami in Turfan where he was welcomed
by the monks. Leaving Hami, he crossed the Tien Shan
into the domain of the Khan who greeted him respectfully.
From there to Tashkent and next to Samarkand where he paused
to study Iranian religion and culture. He crossed the Oxus
to visit some monasteries, continued through the Khyber Pass
to Peshawar, explored the Swat valley and the Indus gorges.

In Kashmir he spent two years studying, then to Patna,
Nalanda and Benares. He crossed the Deccan, went north
along the Bay of Bengal and received an invitation
to Assam, with whose king he traveled up the Ganges.
At last he decided the time had come to start home.
Many years after leaving China Hsüan-tsang returned,
and all of the relics and treasures he had gathered
he gave to his monastery. Only one thing grieved him.
Somewhere in the Punjab he lost several manuscripts
and a collection of flower seeds. Whether or not
the doubts that prompted him to start traveling
were quieted, we'll never know. It seems unlikely.
And what we learn from his adventure is at best
indefinite—perhaps only that a few seeds or a story
can be important.

By the way, if you're planning a trip to India
you might like to know that travelers on the road
between Delhi and Agra are safe from the threat of
strangulation, provided they are water carriers,
oil vendors, carpenters, musicians, washerwomen,
smiths, street sweepers, professors of dancing
or poets.

In Bengal, incidentally, a slave girl can be bought
for a single gold *dinar* or 2½ Magrevinian.
Plump doves are 15 to the *dirhem*. Given a choice,
which would you select?

The poet Gorostiza, asked what he wanted,
wanted nothing so much as an orange—an orange,
a full ripe orange shaped like a human heart.

Lord Adrian, the scientist, wanted the eye of a toad.
If this sounds odd, listen to what he did with it:
he connected the eye to an amplifier and a loudspeaker
so that the retina caught his image as he walked around,
and the alternating patterns of light in his laboratory
produced a sequence of audible clicks.

A devout New England physician, Dr. Duncan Mac Dougall,
desirous of weighing the Soul, ordered moribund patients
trundled onto a hospital scale—observing when they died
a loss of weight that varied from ⅜ oz. to 1½ oz.
Unkind critics, as expected, made other observations.

Jonathan Edwards, a celebrated Puritan,
desirous of fanning the sputtering fire
of Calvinism, retreated to the Berkshire hills
to meditate and to reformulate a doctrine
that should stand as immutably for the future
as for his own day against weakness of spirit.
Master of logic, relentless in analysis,
his tracts on Free Will, Original Sin
and True Virtue persuasively annihilate
forgotten adversaries. With what diversity
we're engaged! Wouldn't you agree?

Mikoíaj Kopernik devoted himself to examining,
reflecting, and theorizing about the sky. On his deathbed
he was shown the first printed copy of a treatise
he had written to summarize his life's work,
and discovered an anonymous editorial preface
which stated that his views should be considered
hypothetical. How bitter to pass through the world
unrecognized. As the French put it: *A bon chien
il ne vient jamais un bon os.*

And how long before I'm appreciated? Day after day
I exhaust myself on my unique problem; night after night
my wife employs her body to weary and deplete me.
How many times I've stuffed my pockets with guineas,
packed a few things, got ready to slip with the tide.
What prevents me? Rectitude. Rectitude, dear friend,
together with the wretched salary I earn.

Arminius Vámbéry has described important ruins
close by the eastern shore of the Caspian Sea
at a place called Gömüshtepe, and a vast wall
with an aqueduct stretching to the mountains

of Persia. Why Vámbéry can visit these places
but I can't, I can guess much too clearly.

I know, of course, that the strength of a woman
is measured by her relentless pursuit of an object.
To incite venery she won't hesitate to use cubebs
steeped in wine like East Indians, or like Africans
the surax root. I know that a woman who's fond of salt
is lascivious: the head of a tortoise when it projects
from the folds of its neck reminds her of a penis
with the foreskin retracted. Every experienced man
looks upon such a woman as he would any natural favor
which, imprudently accepted, could be his undoing.
I also know how predisposed I am to pleasure;
what puzzles me is why I wasn't cautious.

The Arabs are correct. *Orett*, their word for Woman
implies nakedness; and *testiculi* means to bear witness
because long ago a man swore by his procr . . .

3:30 A.M. says the church clock.
Should get a little sleep.
Rain and more rain.
What a long winter this has been,
yet I don't begrudge it. If I live till August
there's no sense complaining. For one thing at least
I'm grateful—I'm rich, thanks to Grandfather.
Still, I'm as obsessed by casualties
and absurdities as my fat body's wracked
by disease. Leisure I have,
excluding hours of pain; relatives
who jump when I ring a silver bell;
everything, in fact, but health
and peace of mind.

Suppose I'd been an alligator,
I might enjoy the situation more;
excitement feeds on itself, they say.
Or suppose I evaporated like a raindrop,
didn't come back for 20 years. What then?

Position filled, death notarized,
wife remarried. Erased from memory.
Everything vanishes, everything passes,
water runs away. Even the heart forgets.

Yesterday my birthday. Got a porcelain vase
with a narrow throat, round and red as a globe,
full of paper curls on which messages were written.
Because the throat of the vase was constricted
I found it impossible to get the messages out,
and it seemed to me that the clamorous voices
were becoming insistent. So, most reluctantly,
I poured water into the vase until they drowned.
What choice had I?

As a rule, I think we're governed by Fate
yet I also believe in the existence of Will
—which isn't as paradoxical as it appears.
For instance, take my son. Home from the Orient
after service with the Army he sits by a window
smoking and smiling emptily at a flower in a gourd.
I doubt if he'd be able to define the word "Ambition."

4 A.M. Fog obscures the bridge. Old and ill I lie here
remembering a girl in Marseille when I was my son's age.
Tout s'en va, tout passe, l'eau coule. Mais le coeu . . .

I remember when I was a child. One Christmas
Grandfather gave me a little ivory walrus
he'd found in the prehistoric city of Ipiutak.
It was ugly and broken, discolored with age.
Dutifully I kissed his cheek and thanked him,
though there was nothing on earth I wanted less.
What I'd hoped to get was a new cap or a cloak
or some white perforated shoes. Unlike my son
I've always been practical.

My wife awoke much distressed a few minutes ago
and said she had dreamt about being followed
by a monkey. I thought if she went for a walk

she might be able to forget. Now I find myself
waiting for the bell to ring and a stranger
who will tell me something horrible,
and say she was seen wandering the streets
followed by a monkey. Dreams, I believe,
offer warnings and indicate the future.

A neighbor of mine who runs a bookshop
went to sleep wrapped in a sheepskin
and dreamt about King Solomon's bowl
in which all manner of devils were kept
—until some Babylonians digging for metals
happened to come across it and let them out.
This dream accounts for the prevalence of Evil.

John Dee dreamt of a variety of books, "bokes"
as he called them, including a volume in quarto
newly printed, with its title on the first page:
Notus in Judaea Deus. He saw many a book, he says,
all filled with strange argument.

In Emmanuel Swedenborg's dream
on the 17th of April, 1744,
he was helplessly bound and cast into Hell.

In my dream I watch German troops
riding toward Amsterdam. I climb a staircase
to a concealed room where I wait and listen:
Alle Joden, die net onverwijld gevolg . . .

Good afternoon. Permit me to introduce myself.
I am a tourist from Düsseldorf. Accompanied by my wife
I stroll along the boulevard just like everybody else,
pausing in front of the tablets only a moment.
Excuse me. You understand, I am sure.

Guten Morgen. Guten Abend. I should like to explain
God suggested numbering those Jews. If you doubt me
read the Second Book of Samuel.

Theresienstadt: 35,000.
This, of course, is an estimate.

Bonjour! Today marks the anniversary of the Huguenot
business when quite a few were chopped up. Roman choirs
sang a *Te Deum*, a medal was struck "in honor of the occasion"
and the Pope himself commissioned an oil painting
to commemorate the final defeat of heresy.

Ciao! Buon gio . . .

In April of 1943 Allied reconnaissance patrols
detected a camouflaged Panzer division
in the ruins of Pompeii. Bombers were called down.
A number of buildings meticulously excavated
and reconstructed by archaeologists
were destroyed forever. The Panzer division,
as you've probably guessed, didn't exist.
A generation later Angkor Wat was bombed
for the same reason. I dislike being obvious,
excuse me.

Aerial bombardment was first introduced to the public
some 60 years ago. I won't bore you with details,
suffice to say that the largest device presently
operational is affectionately referred to by Americans
as a "Cheeseburger." It weighs 8 tons. Too sizeable
for conventional bombers, it must be stowed in the belly
of a cargo plane. A multiwheeled hydraulic lift
manned by a crew of 6 is required to hoist it aboard.
I could describe what happens when the thing explodes
but you get the idea.

There seems to be a bit of a disparity between
Japanese and American estimates of the numbers
obliterated at Hiroshima. 200,000 say the first;
66,000 at most, say the second. Take your choice.

It was Dr. Oppenheimer's opinion that in some crude sense
which no vulgarity, humor or overstatement could extinguish

those physicists responsible for developing atomic weapons
had experienced Sin. Oppenheimer's teacher, Dr. Bridgman,
replied that this was ridiculous; no scientist is liable
for natural facts. It's a scientist's job to uncover facts,
and if anyone should have a feeling of Sin it must be God
who creates fact.

God is the spirit of Light engaged on our behalf
in conflict with the spirit of Darkness, some say;
others perceive creation and destruction as aspects
of principles beyond the limit of human comprehension.
Half-awake, bewildered, how should we decide?

And is it not difficult to recognize one another
among the shifting images of obsessive dreams?
I seem to behold Captain Ernest Medina riding
triumphantly through the streets of Montrose
in a motorcade before his trial for atrocities,
waving to the enthusiastic crowd as if he were
Alexander entering Persepolis.

Tell me frankly: do you think the Universe
is unfolding as it should?
Or perhaps in your opinion
everything works out for the best.

The Commandant of United States Forces in Vietnam
despatched a congratulatory message to the company
responsible for My Lai. How much he knew about it
he alone knows. The official brigade account mentions
14 enemy troops killed, 3 rifles captured. Nothing else.
Consequently, address him as General William Blameless
if you like. I choose not to.

General Order No. 10620, issued October 28, 1970,
by the United States Army cites 21 soldiers
for meritorious service in connection with military
operations against a hostile force from January
to November. Among those receiving the Bronze Star
was a dog: Griffin M. Canine, 096-31-3225, SSG HB,
3rd Bn, 13th Fld Arty, 25th Infantry Division.

Mit der Dummheit kämpfen Gotten selbst vergebens.
Are we expected to know everything?

Ask me whatever you please; I've got 4,321 answers.
Why did Montenegrins chop off the heads of Turks?
In order to carry them around by a lock of hair
or by the moustache.

Why did melons grow on the burial ground in winter
during the reign of Shih Huang Ti? So many executions
warmed and fertilized the soil.

All right, this one's difficult. Dr. Klaus Schilling
infected Jews with malaria. Why? To devise a serum.
Unfortunately, the war ended a little too soon.

Why were plants unknown to British botanists
sprouting from Nazi bomb craters in London?
Because thermal action of the explosions created
metamorphoses in the seeds and genes of pollens.
But why were the implications of this concealed
or distorted by government spokesmen in America
and England? The policy speaks for itself.

Jung postulates an archetypal Wise Man,
an intercessor or mediator lying dormant
in our Unconscious, who has always been there
and wakens when the times grow out of joint,
or society commits itself to a grievous mistake.
If so, how much longer are we expected to wait?

Look. Managua and Hanoi were devastated simultaneously
—one by an earthquake, the other by American bombers.
Nixon sent help to the first, an ultimatum to the second.

Pentagon officials have explained with repressed
annoyance that the Vietnamese seem willing to die
beyond our willingness to kill, which is the source
of all our troubles. I must admit this calls forth
Tertullian's paradox: *Credo quia absurdum est.*

What next? Burton asked leave to establish before us
a stupend, vast, infinite ocean of incredible madness
and folly—a sea of shelves and rocks, sand, gulfs,
Euripuses and contrary tides clogged with monsters,
uncouth shapes, roaring waves, tempests and Siren calms,
Halcyonian seas, unspeakable misery, such Comedies
and Tragedies, such preposterous ridiculous feral and
lamentable fits that he knew not whether they were more
to be pitied or derided, or be believed. Daily we see
these practiced—fresh examples, new extravagance,
objects of misery and madness represented.

Listen. A despatch from the Ben Cui rubber plantation
lists 86 attackers dead, none of our own. Is it true
that we lie in every language, even to ourselves? if so,
to what wild purpose?

Perhaps some faculty within our hearts enables us
to accept illusions and phenomena unrelated to actuality.
Under hypnosis a subject may be persuaded that something
or someone in full view does not exist; he will contrive
fantastic arguments to discredit reality.

In a darkened room if a stationary point of light
is enclosed by a luminous outline which slowly moves,
it appears to us that the static light is moving
and the moving outline is motionless.

Or take the Möbius strip, which illustrates how points
presumably some distance apart might be contiguous.
Of course this suggests a shortcut through the universe
if the geometry of space does indeed prove variable.
But it also suggests analogies with human behavior.

Look. I appreciate your impatience
with what must seem intolerably circuitous;
it's just that affairs of supreme urgency
like root-bound plants send out tentacles
in a dozen directions.

Do you remember the Statements? The Promises?
Or have you forgotten?

Let me remind you: the United States is obligated
by a multiplicity of treaties, some secret,
to assist in the defense of 48 nations
whenever any one of them appeals for help
—or if the Pentagon considers intervention advisable.

Perhaps you know this, but an unspecified quantity
of a gas designated "G-B" has been manufactured.
Theoretically, 300 gallons would be enough
to blot out one billion people.

Look, I had two sons. One was killed in Asia,
the other's lost his wits. I regard them as tokens
in a merciless game of incredible complexity
played for the most part by companies of footmen
snatched from the board by mounted knights, bishops
and other powerful opponents who are supervised
from far away by an immured and terrified king.
Tell me, did they have much chance?

P-B4.
PxP.

Life is tedious and short;
bodies are slow to develop,
but decay is prompt.

As far as I'm concerned, neither Francis
Cardinal Spellman nor Peter the Hermit
should be permitted to lie unmolested.
I have no hesitation about cursing them
in the language they know best: *Et in
verticem ipsius iniquitas ejus descendet!*

I curse the old man who waits furiously for death
beside a river in Texas. Damn him. May his soul rot.
I curse his sycophants' children, let them struggle.
Faithless in one respect, I say, faithless in all.

Wherever my enemies take up their position
I recognize them, regardless of disguise,
and attack them without remorse.
I know next to nothing about ancient coinage,
trade routes, tree rings, skull measurement
or pottery manufacture; but the sputter of rotors
is familiar, and I have seen flares descend
on native villages in the middle of the night.
I'm nobody's fool.

I've heard Colonel Giteau explain the situation
so many times I've lost count. He's persuasive,
I admit, and his argument rings with logic;
it's just that now I'm able to mouth his speech
before he speaks.

Listen. Let me play his words backward:
How much fire we poured into the hamlet
I don't know. It lasted several hours.
Daybreak we started moving downhill.
There was a girl maybe eleven years old
with both arms broke. Hazelwood did her in.
They give us orders to waste everything.
We wasted hogs, buffalo, just whatever
we come across, everything that walked
or swum or fl . . .

I'll try to rearrange this. During the Middle Ages
the earthly and heavenly Jerusalems grew so intermingled
in people's minds that they believed the Pope's appeal
meant Paradise could be seized by force.

Let me be more specific. Byzantine emperors
rode into battle carrying a sword in one hand
and an icon of the Virgin in the other.

Maybe it could be expressed like this: Egyptian banners
rippling from the towers of Christendom's holiest city
so enraged the Crusaders that within a couple of days
they had butchered 40,000 citizens. Such a spectacle

of bodies offered itself and the bloody river flowed
so broad, William of Tyre remarks, that after a while
the soldiers themselves were sickened and disgusted
and flung aside their weapons.

I assume that what I've said is decipherable. If not
this might clarify the matter. As Manuel Comnenus
approached, Reynald de Châtillon considered it expedient
to beg his pardon for having murdered so many Moslems.
He therefore came to the Emperor's tent as a suppliant
without sandals and prostrated himself in the dust.
But the Christian Emperor raised him, kissed his lips
and forgave him. I, myself, am somewhat less charitable.
I'm reluctant to forgive anyone, I refuse adamantly
to overlook what I think is evil, and in my opinion
silence implies consent.

Now, insofar as your intellectual superiority
seems evident, might I beseech you to demonstrate
the use of that magic flail which enables you
to separate wheat from useless chaff?
In other words, I submit the following
questionable statements to be either
accredited or rejected, at your convenience:

Americans are citizens of a maleficent nation.

Bees, if they violate the laws of their king,
kill themselves.

Camels won't swim, but are willing to float.

Devils dress in black and yellow—black for death
and yellow for the livery of quarantine.

Events begin when their time has come,
never sooner.

Fruit may be found among the leaves of books
as readily as women pluck pears from trees.

Gold is meaningless to savages,
who prefer brilliantly colored feathers.

Hubris is arrogance, born of pride
to compound our problems.

Ideas wheel in spreading flocks like birds,
or roll systematically forward
like deep sea waves.

Janizaries are unwilling soldiers.

King Aethelred was chastised by his mother
with a lash of candles.

"Lost Illusions" is every book's title.

Martyrdom is the most complete imitation of Christ,
the most intimate conceivable union with God.

Nero's failure to govern successfully
can be ascribed to a passion for excess,
such as illuminating his gardens at night
with the flaming bodies of crucified Christians.

Odin, Henir and Lodur created Mankind.

Plotinus was so ashamed to live within a body
that he forbade sculptors to record it.

Quod scripsi, scripsi.
I could go on indefinitely
but I exhaust myself.
Tomorrow perhaps
I'll present such riddles,
theses, conundrums,
charades, stupefying
fragments and acrostics
that only serious fools
would presume to answer.

For nothing relating
to any of us can be alien.

Our history commences with Azilian,
the oldest organized language,
which dates back 17,000 years
and is twice as old as Sumerian;
civilization opens with Atl . . .

There are, of course, those who consider
Atlantis fictitious; but on the North Sea floor
Jurgen Spaneth located vestiges of the circular wall
which enclosed its capital, Basilia.

I realize how skeptical you must be. All right,
listen. Tachylite is a vitreous lava which is formed
only in the air, never under water, and decomposes
within 15,000 years. Now, in a Paris museum are fragments
of tachylite culled from the Atlantic north of the Azores
at a depth of 1,000 fathoms.

Here's additional proof. The *Dolphin*, an American ship
working with the German frigate *Gazelle* and the British
Hydra, *Porcupine* and *Challenger*, mapped the Atlantic bed
and reported a mountainous ridge extending from England
to the South American coast at Cape Orange, from there
in a southeasterly direction almost to the African coast
and then as far south as Tristan da Cunha. Significantly,
this now submerged bridge joined the new and old worlds.

Ptolemy bequeathed us the names of five cities
in Armenia: Chol, Colua, Zuivana, Cholima and Zalissa.
Here are the names of five ancient American cities:
Chol-ula, Colua-can, Zuivan, Colima and Xalisco.

Ceramics of coastal Ecuador, circa 3,000 B.C.,
look very much like Jōmon pottery of that period
from southern Japan.

Sandals on the feet of Chacmool at Chichen Itza
are exact replicas of the sandals worn by Guanches
on the Canary Islands.

The more we study, the more elaborate the puzzle.
Explain, if you can, how Martin Behaim in 1492
could have constructed a globe delineating not only
those countries familiar to Europeans but a huge island
west of Iceland. Incidentally, Dithmarus Bleskenius
describes Iceland as a place where the inhabitants
eat fish instead of bread, drink much whey and water
and live 250 years! But the question troubling us
is how Behaim knew of America. Oh, you might say,
it isn't mysterious, probably he was drawing Greenland
which the Vikings had discovered centuries earlier.
But I think the famous geographer knew about Vinland,
Wineland, New England—call it what you like.

How long some slight knowledge of Greenland persisted
we can't be sure, except that during the 13th century
Emperor Frederick II must have known its position.
De arte venandi cum avibus, concerning falconry,
which he wrote, appeared on or about the year 1250
praising the deadly hunting of Greenland's white falcon.
During the 14th century Bernard of Ortolis, papal nuncio,
issued a receipt for a shipment of walrus tusks
contributed to the Church by Greenland settlers.
Beyond this date we make our way slowly. Darkness
closes. Deep fog, frigid winds and the word BRUMAE
stretching in capital letters across Renaissance maps
speak laconically of adventurous men.

Brooding over the entire world and its enigmas
a forgotten genius at the court of the Norwegian king
700 years ago wrote for the edification of his prince
the great *Konnungsskuggsja*, in which we read:
You should understand that the earth is spherical
and not equally close to the sun at all points.
Its curved orbit . . .

Many centuries before this anonymous Norwegian, Egyptians
deduced the earth's spherical shape from a shadow.

Enea Silvio Piccolomini, Pius II, declared in 1461
that knowledgeable men agree on the form of the earth,
if nothing else. *Mundi formam omnes fere consentiunt
rotundam esse.*

Democritus of Abdera, having contemplated the space
beyond the moon, thought it might be filled with stars
too little for anybody to see whose united light
could be responsible for the shimmering ribbon
of our galaxy, and there might well be other worlds.

Bruno argued that the stars were distant suns
and God is a unifying spirit. For such heresies
he was excommunicated and burnt at the stake.

How many of us have been born ahead of time
and how far? Babbage, I'm told, was not one
but two technical revolutions in advance.

My mentor Paracelsus, searching for the origin
of monsters, revealed their hiding place
in the labyrinths of imagination. I, myself,
while quick to admit that I lack my teacher's
perceptivity, have been responsible for occasional
minor elucidations. It would be immodest
to mention them, however I don't mind boasting
that in some respects he and I are similar.
Both of us enjoy writing lengthy chapters on
whatever excites us, and for temporal matters
neither of us holds much affection. Unlike him
I'm blind, but this could be fortune in disguise:
I'm not readily beguiled by the unnatural faces
people paint over their natural expression.

I've learned, not without anguish,
that time spent on anything except study
is wasted, which is why I employ a secretary

to accompany me everywhere and to read aloud,
regardless of what I happen to be doing
—taking a bath, eating my breakfast
or whatever. Life comes sharply into focus
under the strong glass of education.
As Sir Thomas Browne has observed:
Knowledge maketh other cycles.

I know most of what's worth knowing.
I know, for example, earth's diameter:
41,851,160' at its thickest.

I know that mummified llamas in Paracas graves
have 5 toes instead of the usual 2.

I know that a seal lying on a pan of ice
leaves an impression of its belly;
and armadillos, although capable of swimming,
prefer to walk if the crossing is short.

The swan, unmelodious in life, I know
sings beautifully at the hour of its demise.

The sparrow, as virtually everyone knows,
has been aptly nicknamed the Devil's Arrow
for betraying Christ in the Garden of Gethsemane.

I know that a bristlecone pine which lives today
in the foothills of the Sierra Nevada mountains
was 3,000 years old when Christ was born;
and Bors saw the sacred vessel dimly,
as though it were draped with a veil,
because his purity was incomplete.

Outward form, I realize, deceives many;
and I have little doubt that astrology,
being based not upon observation
but altogether upon analytical deduction,
occupies an intermediate position
between medicine and theology.

Chaldean astrologers, I have discovered,
disregarded the effects of stars and planets
upon human activities. This surprised me.

Melancholiacs, I was informed yesterday, can be soothed
by sweet airs played on a hellebore flute; lymphatics
can be cured by brisk airs played on a holly instrument;
flutes made of iris stem or of larkspur cure impotence.

Maniacal furies must be subdued by force, I was taught,
without regard to their cause. All other remedies fail
because violence accedes only to strength, just as poison
cannot be separated from its antidote. Proof of this
lies everywhere from the filthy asylum at Bicêtre
to the coast of China.

Perhaps I take too much on faith; nevertheless
I think truth sooner or later impinges
on our consciousness as surely as explorers
draw sustenance from maps, or legends nourish philosophers.

Very little, I am convinced, do we gain by sharp leaps;
like evolution, discovery is gradual. *Natura
in operationibus suis non facit saltus.*

Very seldom, I believe, do the mind's glorious resources
reveal themselves; perhaps once or twice
in each lifetime.

Necessarily, I think,
we should avoid idiomatic speech
when applying ourselves to timeless subjects.

Babel's many tongues, by the way,
were the many languages of prisoners of war
who labored to construct the tower.

The abject patience of the oppressed, evidently,
is one of history's inexplicable facts.

I've heard, although I've been unable to verify it,
that certain countries generate superior slaves
not only temperamentally but vocationally;
thus prices vary according to origin
and sellers announce their chattel's nation.
Seneca, in any event, is persuaded that slaves have souls
which may closely resemble the souls of free men.
This sounds implausible. What would you say?

Here's a demonstrable fact. The capacity
of the Circus Maximus was 385,000.
More instructive is this: Roman amphitheaters
during the Middle Ages were often used as barns,
and crops were planted in the ancient arenas,
and farmers were astounded by the prodigious growth
—unaware that the earth had been steeped in blood.
Now tell me, what changes? Anything?

At a time when Rome was collapsing
beneath the assaults of barbaric tribes
Christians objected to service in the Legions.
Would you say that sounds familiar?

Well, these have been a few grains
from my warehouse. Devour them, disseminate them,
do as you please. *Wenige wissen, wieviel
man wissen muss, um zu wissen,
wie wenig man weiss.*

5:30 P.M. Legends grow mixed
and distorted. All I know with certainty
is that an hour of apprehension opens with the advent
of darkness. *Videmus nunc per specul...*

Sir John Mandeville claims there's a kind of serpent
in Italy by which men prove whether their children
are bastards. If a child is the result of lawful marriage
the serpent leaves it alone, though if made in avoutry
the snake strikes! But I've witnessed stranger things.
I've seen snakes instantly die when dropped into a jar

containing a sapphire, the mummies of 40 Egyptian kings
in a cave at Deir el-Bahri, a Cambodian leper colony
bombed by Americans, fragments of the Noachic Ark
embedded in a glacier on the south slope of Mt. Ararat
and other sights so extraordinary that if you saw them
you would rub your eyes in disbelief.

I have seen the Emperor of Constantinople
humbly till his fields, albeit with a golden plough;
Phrygians sell their own children into captivity;
knights and barons kneel among the candles,
redolent of incense, while outside the church
spread reeking puddles of blood. I swear, my friend,
there's not much I have yet to see.

Listen. I visited a village in Provence
where seven brothers lived with seven sisters,
and together raised a huge joyful family
until they were all impaled on spikes.

In Würzburg village those convicted of malefaction
customarily were beheaded in groups of four and nine,
though why these numbers were considered significant
I have no idea. All I can tell you is that granted
sufficient time we explore each possibility. Anyway
you might be interested in a list of the doomed:
A musician. Frau Höcker. The widow of old Ancker.
Two strange women. The fat seamstress. The brush-maker.
A strange man. Frau Bentz's daughter. Frau Bentz.
The court smith. Silberhaus. A woman. The spinster
Leibner aged 24. A boy aged 12. The mother
of two sisters. Her daughters. A boy aged 11.
Another boy of similar age. Secretary Schellhar's
wife. Another boy of 12. The maid Bebel
who was beautiful. The steward. Two sons
of the duke's cook. A blind girl.
An old woman. A student who could speak
many tongues and played the harp.
A little deaf ch . . .

Pilgrims granted audience with Pius IX,
who was endowed with the Evil Eye,
averted their gaze during his blessing
for fear he might inadvertently blight them.
Might it not be true, as Whitehead claims,
that nothing could be more incompatible
with Christianity than Christian theology?

Leo X, reflecting on the fable of Christ,
exulted over the lucrative properties it bought.
Decipimur specie recti.

Look. Priests profit by saying mass for the dead,
so they put lighted candles on the backs of tortoises
and release them in cemeteries to wander aimlessly
among the tombstones like earthbound spirits.
Mirabile visu.

A fresh wind may be heard rising across the world,
some say. Others assert that nothing can ever change:
the more it changes, the more it resembles itself.
We shall see secular crowns melt, say the first,
together with the Pope's glittering triple diadem
as irrevocably and swiftly as pagan bronzes were melted
to be resurrected in the shape of Christian cannon.
Plus ça change, plus c'est la même! reply the others.
Now which contention will prove correct, or how soon
some verdict might be handed down for our edification
it would be foolish to predict. By our premises
we're known, and everybody has a theory.

Sophisticates insist that the so-called "Israelites"
who crossed the Red Sea were Viking marauders. Nonsense!
Gullible savages maintain that a race of giants
once inhabited the earth, and you can still see their bones.
Ridiculous! Those are the skeletons of dinosaurs.

On the other hand—well, listen. Naturalists
had great fun with Marco Polo's report of the roc
and not one would travel to Madagascar to investigate.

Only after a number of natives had appeared in Mauritius
with shells as big as buckets did European laughter
begin to sound somewhat reedy. By then, however,
the fabulous bird had been exterminated.
Nothing was left but lifeless eggs
and a few scattered feathers.
Isn't that a good joke?

Here's another. Early in the 18th century
on Guadeloupe Island some goats were released
to forage and multiply, and later to serve as meat
for the crews of whaling ships—a sensible idea
with unanticipated results, because the goats multiplied
as expected but kept right on multiplying
and multiplying and multiplying and ate everything
and then began to starve. The birds flew away
and seals that had always lived along the coast
decided to set up housekeeping someplace else.
In short, if you visit Guadeloupe Island these days
you can amuse yourself by counting polished rocks!

Here's one more. Listen. Captain James Cook
in the name of His Majesty King George the Third
laid claim to South Georgia Island forever
by unfurling the Union Jack
and firing a volley of musket shots
in the general direction of the antipodes
before an audience of mildly interested penguins.

This is the last entertaining story I'll tell.
People used to believe fossils were relics of animals
or of plants drowned in The Flood; or perhaps,
nourished by some occult process, they developed
in the bowels of the earth; or had been sown by Satan
to mislead the faithful; or, not impossibly,
they represented the Lord's first crude experiments.
Now, in Bavaria there was a rather tedious professor
named Johann Beringer who came across several fossils
containing what were apparently archaic Hebrew words
together with illustrations of the sun and the moon.

Very much excited, he wrote a scholarly monograph
describing them and speculating on their origin.
But not long after the publication of his treatise
Beringer dug up a fossil with his name on it.
Undergraduates, of course, had molded and baked
and lovingly buried these little masterpieces
where he'd be sure to find them. Poor Beringer
is reputed to have spent the rest of his life
in bookshops searching for copies of the monograph
which would have been his ticket to immortality,
buying and destroying them one after another.

Here's a curious incident. On August 10th, 1628,
a gentle breeze blew down from the Södra Mountains
filling the sais of the new Swedish warship *Vasa*
on her way to Älvsnabbem. To everybody's surprise
the *Vasa* tipped over, water surged through her ports,
and while thousands watched from the wharves
Sweden's pride grandly sank in Stockholm Strom.
Well, as is customary when these things occur
a court martial was convened to determine the cause
and assign the guilt. Master ship's carpenter
Hein Jacobsson declared himself innocent;
after all, he had paid close attention to the plans
drawn by the masterbuilder Henrik Hybertsson.
Hybertsson could not be summoned, unfortunately,
because he was dead. In any case, King Gustav himself
had approved the design. Nor were the ship's officers
guilty, nor anyone else. Could it have been the wind?

The skeletons of a dozen sailors were recovered
when the *Vasa* eventually was raised in 1961.
Bits of clothing still clung to the icy bones:
knit trousers, heavy wool vests, sandals,
sewn stockings and so forth—typical gear.
But one of these sailors had been a sport;
when he went down he was wearing a linen shirt
beneath an elegant jacket with long sleeves,
and a leather money bag dangled at his waist.
No doubt he had fast plans for the girls

when the voyage ended, although the coins
in the bag combined with those in his pocket
amounted to just 20 *öre.*

Now I'll tell you about the boy-king Tutankhamen
and his child wife. As you've probably heard,
when Carter ordered the slab lifted from its bed
and got his first look into the sarcophagus
he was disappointed because nothing was visible
except a nest of musty gray linen shrouds.
But after these were unrolled he saw an effigy
—the splendid anthropoid coffin 7' long
resting on a bier carved in the shape of a lion.
Two magnificent winged goddesses, Neith and Isis,
were clasping the body of the coffin, wrought in gold
upon gesso, as brilliant as when they were drawn.
The boy's hands and features were sculpted in gold.
The hands, folded across the breast, grasped
Egypt's royal emblems, the Crook and the Flail,
both encrusted with blue faïence. The eyes
were represented with aragonite and obsidian,
the lids and brows inlaid with lapis lazuli;
and on this recumbent figure's forehead
two other emblems had been delicately incised:
the Cobra and the Vulture, symbolizing two Egypts.
All of these riches might have been expected
or at least imagined, but there was something else:
a withered wreath.

Like Scheherazade, I could relate story after story
after story, each successively more marvelous.

Do you know about the diver Elias Stadiatis?
Hunting for sponges in the lee of Antikythera
while waiting for an Aegean storm to subside
he discovered the hulk of a Greek cargo vessel
that must have foundered during a similar storm.
And Stadiatis' companions at the surface saw him
rising like a god through the vitreous depths
holding a marble arm from the age of Pericles!

I could tell you about the dreadful Jamaican earthquake
when several hundred people dropped into fissures.
Some were squeezed to death while those less fortunate
remained alive but helpless, only their heads showing.

I might tell you about a phantom archipelago
descried at twilight west of the Canary Islands.
Unusual atmospheric conditions account for it,
say the authorities; others explain this phenomenon
differently, each according to his temperament.

I know about the cliff dwellings at Puyé,
black with the smoke of primeval fires; Sabina
Poppaea's amber-tinted hair; the lantern dangling
from the end of the long stick Dulle Griet carries;
the world's boundary at Mt. Demavand; leaves blowing
beneath a smoky Paris sky; years dried and curled;
skaldic verse. And that's just a beginning.

In my effort to divine the meaning of the universe
I've traveled, analyzed fables, loved once or twice
and have read 64,138 books. Now, what this means
is that I've had very little time for reflection.
Thus I confuse the true and false, equate curiosity
with significance and mistake knowledge for wisdom.
So much the worse.

If you find yourself either troubled or exasperated
by my pseudonyms, postures and elaborate disguises
remember that this has been a private testament
made of odd details with a touch of the commonplace.
And as we are human, in greater or lesser degree
born of similar experiences, I find myself so like you
that I pause to wonder at such a coincidence.
Do you feel the same?

Well, my friend, whether or not you choose to reply
we've accumulated a quantity of thoughts and events
worth classification. Suppose we register first,
because this was the foulest night of an evil year,

those U.S. soldiers in Vietnam whose features
Hieronymus Bosch delineated five centuries ago.
List them just beneath the rulers responsible,
whose names ought not to be forgotten: Johnson,
Rusk, McNamara, Bundy, Rostow, Nixon, Laird, etc.
Parenthetically, you might mention the *satyagrahi*
whose nature exacts from him implicit obedience
to the highest known law—that of conscience.

State that every particle of matter in the universe
has some attraction for every other particle.

I suggest that you write with colored ink
what we are taught by K'ung fu-tzü:
Each of us is meant to rescue the world.

By all means put down how human life looks
through a teleidoscope, the magnitude of Sirius,
that insoluble problem the Areopagites evaded,
monarchs' games together with monkish dreams,
the latit—ah, but I think your good judgment
should suffice. These were merely a few things
I'd note. All else I leave to your favorable
censure with such submissiveness as I consider
appropr . . .

> *Cetera-desunt.*
> The rest is missing.